Implementing Virtual Reference Services

D1602759

Implementing Virtual Reference Services

A LITA Guide

Edited by

Beth C. Thomsett-Scott

An imprint of the American Library Association

CHICAGO   2013

BETH C. THOMSETT-SCOTT is currently the engineering librarian at the University of North Texas Libraries. In her previous role as reference unit manager, Thomsett-Scott assisted with establishing the libraries' Meebo service, as well as their chat and text messaging services. She has been with the UNT Libraries for ten years with previous positions held at the University of Guelph and University of Western Ontario Libraries. She holds a BS, MS, and MLIS from the Universities of Guelph, Manitoba, and Western Ontario respectively. Thomsett-Scott has served in various positions in professional associations including the American Library Association, Special Library Association, and the Texas Library Association. She has published in a variety of journals and presented conference sessions in the areas of website usability, mentoring and training reference staff and students, and technology. Her passions include virtual reference, website usability, user satisfaction studies, and technologies for reference, instruction, and liaison.

Printed in the United States of America

17 16 15 14 13   5 4 3 2 1

Extensive effort has gone into ensuring the reliability of the information in this book; however, the publisher makes no warranty, express or implied, with respect to the material contained herein.

ISBNs: 978-1-55570-899-3 (paper); 978-1-55570-950-1 (PDF); 978-1-55570-951-8 (ePub); 978-1-55570-952-5 (Kindle). For more information on digital formats, visit the ALA Store at alastore.ala.org and select eEditions.

Library of Congress Cataloging-in-Publication Data
Implementing virtual reference services : a LITA guide / Beth C. Thomsett-Scott, editor.
          pages   cm. — (LITA guides)
     Includes bibliographical references and index.
     ISBN 978-1-55570-899-3
     1. Electronic reference services (Libraries) 2. Electronic reference services (Libraries)—United States—Case studies. I. Thomsett-Scott, Beth C., editor of compilation. II. Library and Information Technology Association (U.S.)
Z711.45.D47 2013
025.5'2—dc23   2012042317

Book design in Berkeley and Avenir. Cover image by ©Pressmaster/Shuttersock, Inc.

♾ This paper meets the requirements of ANSI/NISO Z39.48-1992 (Permanence of Paper).

As my first book, and hopefully just one of more to come, I dedicate this to my God, who brought me to this point and gives me everything I need.

To my mother, who raised me to know that I could do anything.

To my grandmother, who gave me my life values.

To my fabulously intelligent and loving daughter, who sustains me every day and continually teaches me that everything is worth investigating.

Peace to all.

Contents

Contents

Preface

Implementing Virtual Reference Services is a work from the heart. Many of the contributors and I spent needless time flailing around in the sea of information concerning virtual (digital) reference services knowing we needed to—and wanted to—implement services at our organizations, but we were unable to find the basic steps to implement the technology. This book is designed to save readers time and effort by providing the basic information on setting up the popular virtual reference technologies. Readers will be introduced to the technologies and the steps to implement them. Information on staffing, training, and assessing the services is provided to offer a full range of knowledge about virtual reference services.

Using the contributed chapter format allows a wider spectrum of technologies to be covered and to include a greater variety of experiences. The first chapter provides an overview of current technologies, with the subsequent chapters focusing on specific products and their implementation and use. Two state/national services are included as examples of collaborative services in addition to discussing the technologies used by the services.

Readers will benefit from the plethora of images that clearly describe how to access and implement the free technologies included in the book. Vendor-provided software will be discussed in as much detail as possible. All chapters provide reference lists, which can be used to follow up on the content for those readers looking for extra information. There is also a Suggested Reading section that lists a variety of starting points for virtual reference systems in general, website usability and design, marketing, user statistics studies, and keeping up with technology.

On behalf of the contributors, I wish all readers the very best of luck in designing and implementing their virtual reference systems.

Beth

Acknowledgments

I appreciate the University of North Texas and the UNT Libraries for providing a position that lets me stretch myself and continually grow professionally. Thanks to my supervisors, past and present, who have allowed me the freedom to try new things. I am indebted to my colleagues at the Discovery Park Library, who support me in my endeavors. Special gratitude to SAS, who continually bombards with me with new ideas to keep me thinking and trying out new technologies. And, of course, much love and appreciation to my family and friends for, well, everything.

Virtual Reference Services
Considerations and Technologies

Beth Thomsett-Scott

Having been a reference librarian for nearly twenty years, I see reference as being the big picture of patron service. Everything libraries do ultimately supports our users to find, access, retrieve, evaluate, and use information—which, of course, is the essence of *reference*. Reference should be intensely proactive. Gone are the days when patrons would dutifully visit library service desks in person and willingly attend every workshop and class instruction opportunity. We need to reach out to our users and provide web-based products and services that are findable and meet their needs. Rather than waiting for a user to ask a question, reference staff should provide help objects—such as class pages and subject guides—and services to assist users with locating answers to their questions without needing to contact a librarian.

Virtual reference (VR), at its simplest, occurs when the patron and librarian are not in face-to-face communication. This includes the times patrons instant message (IM) a librarian even though they are at the public terminal closest to the reference desk. Depending on the definition of *virtual*, mail, fax, and phone reference are considered to be part of the VR suite of options. At one time, the terms *digital* or *electronic reference* were used as well, but the most popular term today is *virtual*. When e-mail was made widely available in the late 1980s, many libraries quickly adopted it as a form of virtual reference. In the late 1990s, with the development of the Virtual Reference Help Desk by LSSI, Tutor.com, and a few other companies, the concept of virtual reference was truly born. Patrons now could chat with library staff while viewing web pages the librarian had selected, and both parties could watch the other navigate these pages online. These high-end services had some

1

issues, such as dropped connections and need for higher-end computers than some users had at the time. Later, many libraries also welcomed the appearance of IM as a new form of reference. The development of text reference and social media tools further added to the wealth of technologies available. However, this wealth also meant that some decisions had to be made. Few libraries were able to offer every single form of virtual reference.

Reference can be performed *synchronously* (in real time) or *asynchronously* (delayed). Face-to-face, telephone, chat, and IM are examples of synchronous reference methods. Popular forms of asynchronous reference methods are text messaging (although hopefully with only a short time delay), e-mail, discussion boards, reference blogs and wikis, and social media tools such as Facebook and Twitter. Taking face-to-face out of the mix, most other methods of reference, whether synchronous or asynchronous, have "channel loss" due to the lack or limited availability of voice, facial expressions, and body language, resulting in the "depersonalization" of the librarian (Dumas and Peterson 2010). Some patrons value the anonymity while others prefer a more personal connection. Several tools discussed below will help with personalizing virtual reference interactions.

In today's libraries, we see continued diversification in terms of age, cultures, nationalities, and learning styles of our patrons. Providing a variety of reference options ensures that every user is able to receive a high-quality response to their question, whether they ask a reference staff member or seek an answer themselves. Any service we offer must be perceived as useful to users in order for them to try it and continue to use it. Thus, it is vital that we meet their needs in terms of timeliness, ease, and convenience. Most important, we must ensure that the information satisfies their request. To do this well, we need to know our users and be willing to experiment with and implement services and technologies that they will use.

IMPLEMENTING OR ENHANCING A VIRTUAL REFERENCE SERVICE

Selecting Technologies

Since national statistics may not always reflect the population and technology characteristics of an organization's stakeholders, it is essential that each organization conduct a needs assessment to the best of its staffing and financial situation. There are several helpful items listed in the Suggested Reading for those interested in learning more about needs assessment and user studies. It is important to choose tools that your patrons will use. The patron culture of each library is different. You may find that your patrons are very different from the "national norm" and that some technologies will work well and others will not ever be popular. Patrons may also differ in their interest is using a technology with regard to the library. Even though a technology may be mainstream in the target population, users may not see the value or have interest in using it to communicate with a reference staff member. Consider the risk/reward ratio for a technology and try as many as you can. If one doesn't work, remove it. Try it again in a year—your patrons may change. However, be sure that the lack of use is not due to poor marketing. Guder (2009) provides an example of Second Life in terms of the diffusion of innovation for technologies; basically, how or why a technology becomes popular. He makes valid points that a technology, among other things, must be useful to the group it is being promoted to, and also be functional within the organization.

Each technology has its own characteristics, requiring us to learn its ins and outs, especially in how to communicate most effectively with our users. Even something as simple as a web page requires that we write in a different way than if we were writing a print document. Ancelet, Fisher, and Spies (2009, 52) say it well: "Every time we implement innovations, especially radical ones, we must learn a new language. In a sense, we are translating our work into a new mode of practice." This statement is very true. It is critical to the success of the service to know the culture of the tool and to adapt our messages to the tool. For example, Twitter is often seen as being more informal, and messages sent through this system need to have an inviting tone while maintaining an appropriate degree of professionalism. Staff may need to be versed on the different communication styles of each tool and have some template messages provided as examples. Depending on the process for the coordination of feeds and updates, the development of standards may be easy or more complicated, especially if several departments have their own accounts. For example, consider the situation in which a library has several departments each with its own Twitter and Facebook accounts. Every department advertises its own events and services, but not general library news. A music library may not want to post about the purchase of a long-awaited science database, but it may want to let their users know that a new information commons is open in the science library. If there is no coordination among the different accounts, important opportunities for reference and overall library services may be missed.

3

Cost

Naturally the cost of any service is extremely important for libraries. There are many free technologies available that are quite stable and provide high-quality service to patrons. However, a pay service can often provide additional features, such as a statistical reporting tool and technical support. Libraries need to balance the return on investment and convenience when considering fee versus free. Factors include availability of library technology help; traffic (lower traffic places less stress on free systems and also becomes less cost-effective for a fee-based system); staff knowledge and interest; uptake of new technologies by patrons; and support from administration.

Staffing

There are several immediate questions when considering staffing. Some libraries prefer that only librarians staff virtual reference regardless of whether or not paraprofessionals staff the physical desk, due to the perceived differences in virtual reference transactions. Virtual reference requires several high-level skills, including the ability to show interest and empathy despite the lack of in-person cues and the necessity of keeping an ongoing flow of conversation while seeking the answer for the patrons. Many experienced paraprofessionals and well-trained students have or can acquire these skills. In the author's experience, those who are interested in providing virtual reference are often better operators than those who are trained yet reticent about the technology.

Another common discussion is whether to staff virtual reference services from the physical reference desk. Often the decision centers on the traffic at the physical desk and the number of virtual services. Smaller libraries with low traffic often find that having an IM service staffed from the physical desk is acceptable. Larger libraries with higher traffic and multiple virtual services find that the virtual services work best staffed separately. Most libraries tend to have one staff member monitor all virtual services during a shift. A good practice is to have a backup in case of heavy traffic, for rest breaks, or for additional knowledge support.

Libraries also need to determine how many hours a week virtual reference will be staffed. This may be based on staff availability, traffic patterns, consortia requirements, and perceived or current use. Other decisions include whether staff will be able to monitor virtual reference from home which is helpful for weekends, holidays, and inclement weather; reduced hours during summers, intercessions, and holidays; to include staff who are not located in the reference department; separate schedule for virtual reference; and length of shift (Meola and Stormont 2002, Ronan 2003). Blonde (2006) noted that two-hour shifts are the most popular. As discussed in chapter 5, "Instant Messaging for Virtual Reference," the University of North Texas permitted staff to work from home on the condition that the time was to be fully used for work. They also incorporated staff from other departments to monitor virtual reference, especially during departmental meetings and poorly staffed times. Since virtual reference transactions are often less detailed than in-person transactions, several nonreference staff felt capable enough to work the virtual reference suite of services. The result was very positive. The staff enjoyed doing something different and their availability greatly assisted with scheduling. Their training was fairly simple; a cheat sheet was created for all staff containing log-in information and tips and tricks for each service. Staff had a basic knowledge of the UNT Libraries catalog and electronic resources. Any patron who had questions requiring an in-depth subject knowledge were asked to provide their e-mail address and a subject librarian would contact them. In this way patrons received quality service from both reference and nonreference staff.

Training

Training discussions frequently cover the full spectrum of options. Staff members who are technologically adept often prefer a quick overview, some hands-on practice, role playing, and then eagerly wait for their first shift. At the opposite end fall those who prefer detailed instruction, lots of hands on, intensive practice as both librarians and patrons, and several shifts of being double-staffed with others for support. Other staff members fall in between these two groups. Abels and Ruffner (2006) researched training preferences for virtual reference technologies and reported that, both in the literature and through their research, most staff prefer a combination of training activities, especially role-playing. Cheat sheets were a popular request. Meola and Stormont (2002) noted that virtual reference training should consist of general reference skills, chat techniques, policy knowledge, and software skills related to the service used. I would emphasize that techniques for each technology are perhaps the most essential—and sometimes the most difficult—part of the training. For example, communicating via Twitter is much different from an interaction in a chat system with page-pushing capabilities.

Marketing

Marketing is one of the most vital elements to a successful virtual reference service yet is often treated as an afterthought. There are a number of great marketing books available. Several of these are included in the Suggested Reading section of this book.

Evaluation and Assessment

Evaluation and assessment are also important components of a successful virtual reference service. Evaluation considers quality of the transactions, accuracy, and user satisfaction (Kern 2009). There are a number of metrics for general assessment including the cost per question (Marstellar and Ware 2006), questions per hour, questions per day, questions per staff member. (Kern 2009). In order to do an effective comparison, the number of questions and the number of transactions need to be clearly presented as there can be multiple questions within a single transaction. Also, reports should clearly indicate which services are being analyzed, as transaction numbers differ depending upon the service used.

Success of transactions is often difficult to measure; factors include not only the accuracy of the answer, but the speed of response, personality of operator, user satisfaction, and quality of resources as well. User satisfaction can be measured by surveys, interviews, and focus groups.

Other measures of overall success include percent of potential population reached, percent of return users, and average transactions over time (Kern 2009). While these numbers may be low, the goal is to see them increase as the service matures.

PATRON ACCEPTANCE OF VIRTUAL REFERENCE

While most libraries have not seen the uptake on the use of their virtual services that they expected, virtual reference services have developed a dedicated base of return users and continue to attract new users. Low numbers can be attributed to a variety of factors; lack of marketing is likely the number-one issue. Although libraries often have a Contact Us page, oftentimes only a small proportion of patrons will seek this page out, and an even smaller proportion take advantage of the services. Additionally, while patrons may make personal use of the technologies, they don't always consider the technologies to be valid for library assistance. As with any service, there are patron expectations, especially for speed and accuracy, that may influence the use or reuse of virtual reference services. Libraries need to incorporate the points above to ensure the most cost-effective service for the library and the most satisfying transaction for the patrons.

SELECTED VIRTUAL REFERENCE TECHNOLOGIES

Web Pages

Although most readers might not think of web pages as being a reference service, web pages are the first "face" of the library for online users. Welch (2005a, 225) referred to websites as "electronic welcome mats." Such items as ready reference pages, subject guides, tutorials, and information pages function as the initial form of virtual reference that our users experience. Items such as online subject/resource/research guides and tutorials function to help our online users; thus, hits on these items should be included as reference statistics (Welch 2005b). This inclusion is not a new idea by any means; however, the idea bears repeating anytime we look to validate our roles to our administrators, especially during difficult economic situations.

Reference questions have declined in general over the years; however, this coincides in large part with the proliferation of library reference and help pages. While it is unlikely that there is a one-to-one effect, it can be interpreted that these pages account for some of the decline of questions at the reference desk, as users learn to serve themselves. Additionally, since the web is available to most people, general surfing for answers also occurs. Library web pages need to have sufficient metadata to force the pages to appear high up in web search results, since we want our patrons to find—and use—the information and services we provide.

In addition to making pages "findable," sites must meet the needs of the user and be appealing. There are many articles and books written on effective website design and usability for readers who are interested in following up on it.. The Suggested Reading section at the end of this book contains several helpful starting resources.

LibraryH3lp

LibraryH3lp (http://libraryh3lp.com) was designed by Pam and Eric Sessoms to allow multiple virtual reference accounts, and increase the ease of transferring questions between departments (Sessoms and Sessoms 2008). LibraryH3lp can be computer-based using a freely downloaded XMPP/Jabber client (Pidgin for

7

Windows or Adium for Mac are good examples), or through a web-based interface available from the LibraryH3lp website (http://libraryh3lp.com/live-librarian-chat/; Evans, McHale, and Sobel 2009). The availability of web access is a tremendous advantage for libraries, as it reduces the impact on systems staff and resources. The software is affordable, and many libraries are very satisfied with the product. LibraryH3lp is used as an integral part of the services provided by the University of Nevada–Las Vegas as described in chapter 6, "Embedded Librarians Using Web 2.0 Services for Reference." This section will focus on general technology and assessment of the product.

Queues are available to allow librarians to transfer patrons to other librarians for more in-depth responses. Transcripts are stored automatically. Statistics are relatively easy to generate. There is a variety of patron options available for use. Patrons can access the system through a widget, send IMs through the various client options, or text using cell phones or other text messaging options. Regardless of where the question originates, all questions appear in one single interface. Widgets are ADA compliant and can be placed on Facebook and LibGuides pages, as well as regular web pages. There are a variety of ways to customize the widgets, and multiple widgets can be developed, allowing separate widgets for each queue (e.g., library department, subject librarians). A recent review of LibraryH3lp highlighted the wealth of documentation and support available, and the willingness of the developers to add enhancements (Evans, McHale, and Sobel 2009). An example of

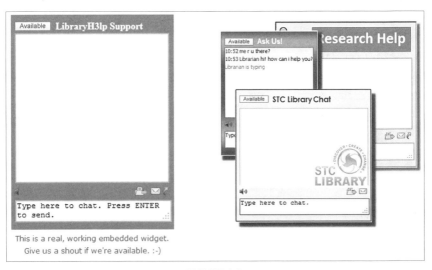

FIGURE 1.1
Samples of Customized LibraryH3lp Widgets

community activity is shown in http://libraryh3lp.blogspot.com/2009/05/facebook
-app.html, which describes, with slides, the process for adding the LibraryH3lp
widget to a Facebook page. Figure 1.1 provides samples of customized widgets as
shown in LibraryH3lp documentation.

Examples of administrative reports from LibraryH3lp documentation are shown
in figure 1.2.

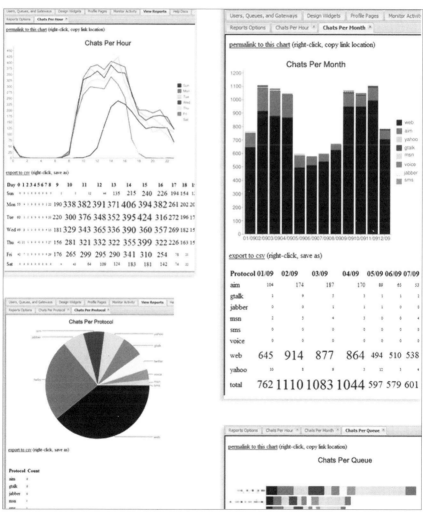

FIGURE 1.2
Samples of LibraryH3lp Administrative Reports

Contact the vendor at http://libraryh3lp.com for additional information. Theiss-White et al. (2009) offer helpful advice for implementing and assessing LibraryH3lp.

LibAnswers

LibAnswers (www.springshare.com/libanswers/) provides automatic generation of a frequently asked questions (FAQ) reference database based on questions that are actually asked by patrons. LibAnswers allows the inclusion of images, videos, and hyperlinks, and the assigning of multiple topics and keywords to answers. Responses can be private or public. Libraries of all types and sizes are using LibAnswers.

There is a fairly nominal cost: at press time, the basic option is between $599 and $1,099 based on full-time equivalent for academic libraries or number of

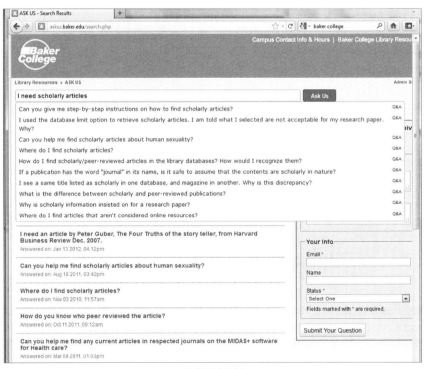

FIGURE 1.3
LibAnswers Search Box—Baker College Library

cardholders for public libraries (Evans 2011). Additional modules exist, such as a module to provide short message service (SMS) capabilities. LibAnswers is a hosted product, minimizing implications for an organization's technical staff.

The patron side provides a basic search box with drop-down responses based on a user's query. Users can choose to view the available responses or send in a question (fig. 1.3). A Share button will send question and answer pairs to Twitter and Facebook (fig. 1.4). While social media and reference have generated many discussions, pro and con, Evans (2011) noted that a recent focus group of students reported that they use social media to share information on library services and resources, and that the share button is a strong reason for them to use LibAnswers. While we might not be "friends" with our users, sharing concise information through social media outlets is a good way to let people know about our services and resources.

FIGURE 1.4
LibAnswers Share Button—Baker College Library

The highly customizable public interface allows IM widgets, links to other services, and more. Widgets and buttons are available to customize and embed on web pages, including most course management systems. A good example of an IM widget is provided in figure 1.5. LibAnswers includes multiple queues and a claiming system that provide a high level of functionality for multiple staff to access. This aspect is a valuable feature for consortiums and librarians at multiple locations who occasionally want to answer location specific questions (Evans 2011). Asynchronous methods of reference such as Twitter, Facebook, and e-mail, and SMS if purchased, are automatically fed into LibAnswers. Synchronous methods such as IM, chat, and walk-up patrons need to be entered manually.

There is a straightforward administrative module with an appealing and easy-to-use interface. The basic reference statistics module is helpful, although the

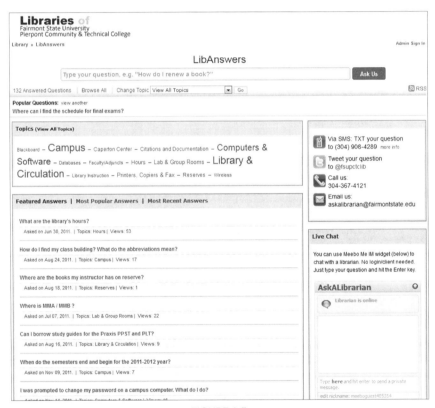

FIGURE 1.5
LibAnswers Chat Widget—Fairmont State University
and Pierpont Community Technical College Libraries

optional LibAnalytics is more powerful (Evans 2011). Another module, QuerySpy, allows staff to see, in real time, questions arriving into LibAnswers and from which technology. Questions that are abandoned by users are also shown. QuerySpy allows library staff to immediately become aware of problems such as "what do I do when X database asks for a password?" or "I need 3 articles on the dust bowl for class xyz."

LibAnswers developers are responsive to issues and suggestions for improvements from users. As an example, the text of library answers is not searchable; thus staff has to be extra diligent at adding appropriate keywords to maximize retrieval (Evans, 2011). The author notes that an enhancement to correct this is in development as is the ability to create mini-FAQs from current LibAnswers responses and include these on web pages, LibGuides, library catalogs, and other locations. As with any FAQ, however, there must be attention to keeping it updated and well promoted.

Contact the vendor (www.springshare.com/libanswers/) for additional information.

13

Text Messaging

Text messaging is covered in chapter 7, "My Info Quest: A National Text Reference Message Service," and mentioned in several other chapters. This section will briefly describe text messaging and provide a few tips for use. Short message service (SMS) is a communications protocol that enables mobile phone users to send text messages to another phone, e-mail, or IM software application. Based on a review of text messaging vendors mentioned on the Library Success Wiki (www.libsuccess.org), popular vendor-based products include Altarama (www.altarama.com/Products/SMSreference/), Mosio's Text a Librarian (http://textalibrarian.com), Upside Wireless (www.upsidewireless.com), and LibraryH3lp (http:// libraryh3lp.com).

For libraries needing a basic solution, text messages can be sent to an e-mail address. Instead of keying in a phone number, the patron types in an e-mail address. Library staff receives the text in their e-mail account, and their response is sent to the patron in the form of a text message. Since most libraries have an account for reference queries, this can be a simple way of offering a text messaging service. Staff will need some training on text messaging replies—in particular the character limitations—if they are not familiar with texting. Trillian (www.trillian .im), among other products, can be used to provide instant notifications to ensure that staff members are aware when a text arrives.

Second Life

Second Life (www.secondlife.com) is an immersive environment released in 2003 by Linden Labs, and has been referred to as the "ultimate vehicle for social networking" (Dumas and Peterson 2010). Offering the ability to chat and use voice, Second Life provides for the personalization of libraries that some virtual reference options have lost. Admittedly, Second Life received a lot of attention between 2006 and 2009 and has dipped in popularity in the library world since then. However, it is included in this chapter as there was a recent Web4Lib (http://web4lib.org) discussion on libraries and information resources in Second Life. There is also an active group of Second Life librarians (www.infoisland.org) and at least one library actively offers reference by appointment sessions in Second Life (fig. 1.6).

There are some thoughts in the literature that Second Life faded in popularity due to the high learning curve and heavy technological requirements. Three library school students guest edited a column on Second Life (Ford et al. 2008). Their experiences support the impression of a steep learning curve, which can be frustrating or disorientating depending on your nature, and requires top-of-the-line equipment and connections. However, they noted that overall the encounters were useful, the avatars provide a sense of community lacking in other digital reference environments, and that there are some excellent sources of real-life reference, such as the HealthInfo Island options. Privacy was a concern, as all text and voice transactions were available to all unless a special one-to-one mode was initiated. The availability of voice was hailed as being highly beneficial to the transaction by all three of the students. One student noted that Second Life would be of more interest if she could pull a book off a shelf and read it in PDF and if there was a way to link a library's holding in Second Life to allow access to databases and e-books. If libraries resume their interest in Second Life as a form of virtual reference, these enhancements will be likely be developed. An excellent review of the literature pertaining to Second Life is provided by Tang (2010).

Guder (2009) discusses Second Life in terms of the diffusion of innovation. While some librarians tend to delve into the newest technology, our patrons and administrators may not; thus, increasing the time before an innovation, such as Second Life, becomes widely acceptable to our stakeholders. Now that most new systems meet the demands of Second Life and high-speed Internet connections are generally the norm, we may see a resurgence of interest in reference services through Second Life. Even if we don't, it is an interesting technology to explore. Depending on your user base and their information-seeking preferences, Second Life may be of interest.

Second Life's home page is located at www.secondlife.com. Click on the Join Now button in the middle of the screen. Select your personal avatar and complete the registration form. Choose either the free or premium edition. Upgrades and additional customization also are available. The Second Life software will download at your request. Log in to begin playing. If you are new to Second Life, it may be

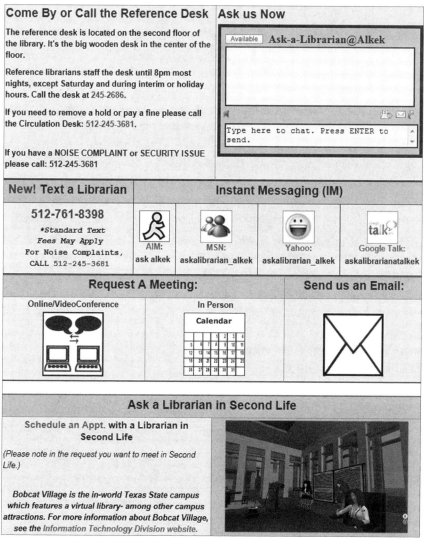

FIGURE 1.6
Life Reference by Appointment—Alkek Library, Texas State University

useful to head to the Virtual Reference Desk on Info Island to orient yourself. Check out the Community Virtual Library's calendar of events at www.infoisland.org.

Skype

Released in 2003, Skype is a popular voice-over IP (VoIP) system that includes video capability. Skype uses a computer's internet connection to communicate with other computers and is compatible with Windows, Linux, and Mac systems.

Skype provides text chat, VoIP, SMS messaging, group chats with other Skypers, and conference calling, as well as standard phone options such as voice mail and call transferring for free. Additional features are available for a cost. File sharing and screen sharing are freely available for one-to-one calls. Images, video clips, text, word processing, and spreadsheets are able to be shared between Skypers. The screen sharing can function as a co-browse tool, similar to some vendor-based virtual reference systems. Skype incorporates a contact list similar to the buddy list of instant messaging systems. This helps users see Skype as familiar. The text chat allows for longer, more detailed messages than available through IM and most SMS systems. This is an advantage for librarians who have been unhappy with the limited space in IM products both for conducting the reference interview and for providing a thorough answer to a reference question. We still have to be aware of our patron's interest in our answers and the tool use; thus a long answer may still be more effective if they are broken into several shorter messages.

Another free tool, PowerGramo (www.powergramo.com) provides the ability to record Skype-to-Skype transactions (Fontichiaro 2008). Upgraded versions of PowerGramo are available for a cost. This feature is helpful for tutorials and for more involved questions that may need review by a subject matter expert or a supervisor. These also provide training opportunities. However, there are some questions with patron privacy. Patrons must be notified that the session is being recorded.

Jing files can be sent through Skype (Gervasio, Bryan, and Steinmann 2010). Jing is a free tool for quick video capture used fairly frequently in libraries as the videos can be sent to the patron as part of a reference transaction. Patrons frequently appreciate the visual aspect of the tutorials.

By combining the power of vendor-based software for screen sharing and file transfer, while keeping the synchronous flow of text or voice and the enhancement of video, Skype almost mimics a face-to-face transaction. Skype is easy to operate, requiring a microphone and speakers. A webcam provides the full effect of personalization but is not necessary. Many libraries take advantage of the video, although this may be too invasive for users, as supported by Booth (2008) who reported that video was rarely used despite the relatively high use of text and/or voice. After Gervasio, Bryan, and Steinmann (2010) conducted a brief survey of 111 users, they reported that 53 percent of the participants would not use Skype to contact a reference librarian. The authors postulated that users might find Skype to be too intimate because of its use of video. However, they question whether Skyping on mobile devices, where the video is less prominent, might increase the use of Skype for reference questions. However, video is not a requirement for Skype and could be made optional for patrons, which might increase its use. Adding voice to the standard IM is still an improvement. Perhaps using Skype as a communication system, similar to IM, may increase its popularity.

From the main Skype page, www.skype.com, click on the Join Skype button at the top right. The form requires a user name, a password, an e-mail address, a phone number, and some general profile information. Once the account is complete, download the required software. There is an option to provide a profile picture. Skype will import contacts using a link to your e-mail account, or you can manually enter the information. Figure 1.7 provides an example of a library advertising Skype. Segerstrom (2007) provides suggestions for setup and effective use of Skype.

FIGURE 1.7
Skype a Librarian—Ohio University Libraries

Twitter

Twitter is discussed in more detail in chapter 2, "Using Twitter for Virtual Reference Services." This section will highlight some advantages, tips, and techniques. Twitter is a form of *microblog*—a micro (or mini) version of its cousin, the standard blog. A recent review of the use of Twitter by libraries shows between 830 and 996 libraries with a Twitter account (Forrestal, 2011). While it is safe to assume that some of these may be inactive, the numbers show a deep-seated interest in Twitter. In fact, a librarian was identified in 2010 as being one of the most influential noncelebrity users of Twitter with few followers but high degree of messages being retweeted, mentioned, or forwarded (Young 2010).

Planning is always an indispensable part of offering a new service. For best results, personalize your Twitter site with pictures or logos, add links to library's website and services, and provide a biography or brief introduction. Match the colors and overall appearance to the organization. The more recognizable and attractive a page is, the more likely users will trust it enough to use it.

Some librarians are concerned about the limitation of characters when using Twitter as a reference tool; however, "Twitter can act as a starting point for greater conversation" (Forrestal 2011, 150). The conversation can be moved to another technology that is more appropriate for the question or for privacy concerns.

Twitter can also be used as a feedback mechanism for libraries to learn how their patrons are using the library, performing research, commenting on library services, and more (Cuddy, Graham, and Morton-Owens 2010, Forrestal 2011). If users post or comment about services or resources, both compliments and complaints can be recorded. Problems can be fixed in a more timely fashion. For example, if a journal article database goes offline, a tweet from a user can serve as instant awareness of the problem. Establishing general feeds for terms such as *research*, *paper*, or *writing* and limited to your local area provides an opportunity to respond without the user directly mentioning the library (Forrestal, 2011). This is an excellent example of anticipating reference questions and providing an answer before the question is actually asked. Filgo provides a variety of ways to encourage followers and to monitor tweets in chapter 2, while Sutton (2010) notes the ten most frequent reasons for a low following. Overall, if used effectively, Twitter can serve as a way to receive reference questions, search for unasked questions or problems, and help libraries interact with their patrons. Figure 1.8 shows an example of an active Twitter stream.

FIGURE 1.8
Twitter Page—Wells Library, Indiana University at Bloomington

Please see chapter 2, "Using Twitter for Virtual Reference Services," for Twitter account setup.

Facebook

Many libraries have Facebook pages, although there is much discussion about how these pages should be used and how patrons should be contacted. Libraries and librarians with professional pages should complete their profile page, list services, include photos or images, and link to relevant pages in order to encourage maximum use of the page. Figure 1.9 shows a well-designed page. Initially intended for individuals, Facebook has adapted its system to allow for organization and topic pages. At first, organization pages had limited functionality compared to a personal account, although Facebook has been fairly responsive to these concerns (Sekyere 2009). The pressing issue for most libraries is that the chat feature doesn't operate on organization pages. Of course, IM widgets can be added to Facebook pages that help overcome the lack of synchronous Facebook chat, although these are extra steps for both the librarian and the user. Some subject or liaison librarians maintain individual pages for professional use that allow them to offer Facebook chat as another option for patron contact, as well as often including personalized widgets. Facebook Insights (www.facebook.com/help/search/?q=insights) allows page owners to see metrics, which can be a useful source of assessment data.

Facebook developers provide for advanced customization through the use of Facebook markup language (FBML). An example of customization is the development of custom tabs, which permits chat widgets to be added on the main page, given their own tab, or put in the boxes tab (Steiner 2009). The application programming interface (API) offers an opportunity to create new applications. Popular applications include catalog searches that users can embed on their pages. Figure 1.10 shows the variety of apps available for Olympic College. LibGuides, the popular subject-resource-guide page service, can be utilized in Facebook via a new application (fig. 1.11). Blogs can be made to automatically feed into Facebook, which provides easy updating of pages (Tagtmeier 2010).

Users tend to prefer to link pages rather than be invited. The majority of students responding to a local survey on Facebook use preferred to be contacted passively by choosing whether to "like" a page and embed the feed rather than receiving invite messages (Sachs, Eckel, and Langan 2011). The survey also showed a high interest in receiving research tips and information about specific resources.

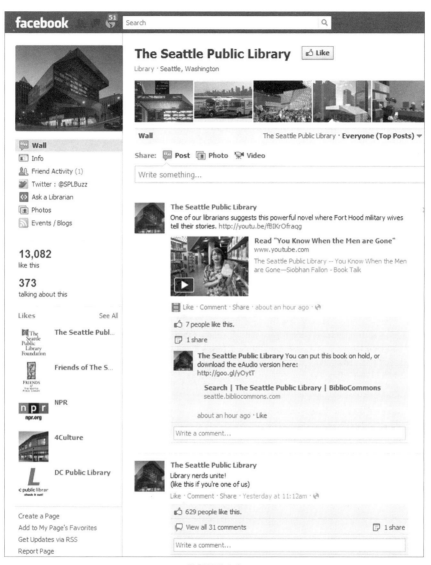

FIGURE 1.9

Facebook Page—Seattle Public Library

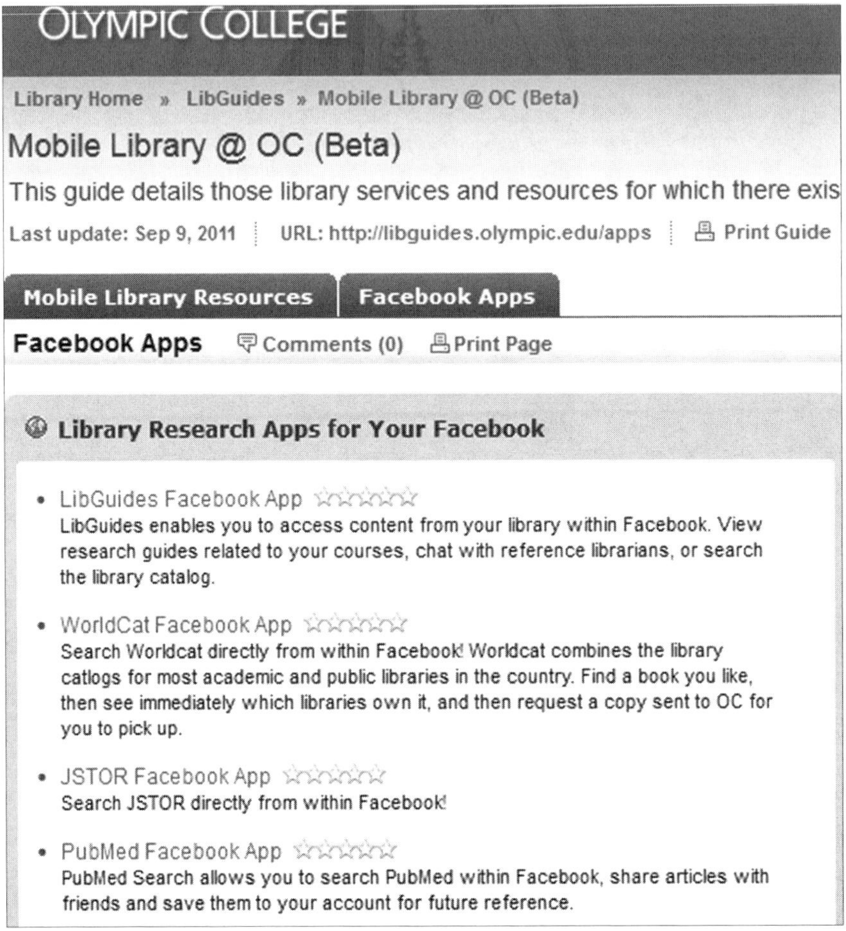

OLYMPIC COLLEGE

Library Home   »   LibGuides   »   Mobile Library @ OC (Beta)

Mobile Library @ OC (Beta)

This guide details those library services and resources for which there exis

Last update: Sep 9, 2011 | URL: http://libguides.olympic.edu/apps | 🖨 Print Guide

Mobile Library Resources | **Facebook Apps**

Facebook Apps   🗩 Comments (0)   🖨 Print Page

⊛ Library Research Apps for Your Facebook

- LibGuides Facebook App ☆☆☆☆☆
  LibGuides enables you to access content from your library within Facebook. View research guides related to your courses, chat with reference librarians, or search the library catalog.

- WorldCat Facebook App ☆☆☆☆☆
  Search Worldcat directly from within Facebook! Worldcat combines the library catlogs for most academic and public libraries in the country. Find a book you like, then see immediately which libraries own it, and then request a copy sent to OC for you to pick up.

- JSTOR Facebook App ☆☆☆☆☆
  Search JSTOR directly from within Facebook!

- PubMed Facebook App ☆☆☆☆☆
  PubMed Search allows you to search PubMed within Facebook, share articles with friends and save them to your account for future reference.

FIGURE 1.10
Examples of Facebook Applications—Olympic College Library

Marketing a Facebook page to individuals during reference or instruction contacts is an effective yet subtle means to build a fan base (Cheney 2010).

Once the page is designed and policies are in place, posting fresh items, responding to comments, and adding new images from events and promotions take very little time. Five to ten minutes a day is generally sufficient. Creating appropriate wording when first offering a Facebook reference page may take a little more time, since posts need to be inviting and friendly, as well as useful. Once one is used to the look and feel of Facebook messages, the process of writing new posts becomes second nature.

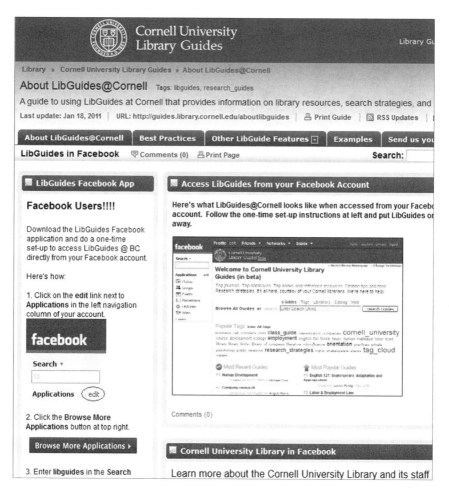

FIGURE 1.11
Facebook and LibGuides—Cornell University Library

From Facebook's home page, www.facebook.com, select "create a page for a celebrity, band, or business" from the lower right-hand side. On the next screen, select which grouping is more relevant (most libraries tend to select Company, Organization, or Institution). Continue through the profile information and customize as desired. Following the advice above, brand your page with your organization's name, colors, and content. Add in your reference options. Seattle Public Library's Ask a Librarian (fig. 1.12) is a good example to follow. Figure 1.13 shows Worchester's Public Library's Quick Reference Facebook page, which is an appealing way of advertising quick reference sources.

FIGURE 1.12
Facebook Ask a Librarian Page—Seattle Public Library

Once the technologies are selected, tested, implemented, and provided to the users, marketing and advertising come into play. There are a number of quality works on the subject of marketing virtual reference (see Suggested Reading for examples). While word of mouth is ultimately the best advertising, libraries need strong marketing programs, especially for new or underutilized services. One good thing to do to market reference services is to include all services on one page, such as an Ask a Librarian or Ask Us page, and briefly highlight the value or purpose for each service (Strothmann, McCain, and Scrivener 2009).

As most of us are aware, the more consistent our brand—including user names—the more recognizable we are to our customers and the more connected our services appear. Additionally, the trust factor comes into play: once a patron has a solid interaction with a chat service, they will be more likely to experiment with a Twitter or IM service. Providing a consistent branding and profile allows users to seamlessly move from one reference service to another (DeVoe 2009). For

FIGURE 1.13
Facebook Quick Reference Page—Worcester Public Library

example, a patron might see a tweet of interest that leads her to a Facebook post, and then to a library page on effective writing for scientific literature reviews. If the branding varies from tool to tool, the patron may wonder whether she is following the correct path or have doubts about the quality of the information. The easier we make it for our patrons to find and recognize us, the more likely they are to trust and use our services and resources.

VIRTUAL REFERENCE SUCCESS TIPS

When selecting names for virtual reference options, keep the name recognizable, not too overly long to be unwieldy and not too short to be unfamiliar. Tools such as KnowEm (www.knowem.com) or NameChk (www.namechk.com) can be used to check for availability of your preferred profile name across various social networking sites. Libraries should maintain awareness of new technologies and claim the usual acronym for their library, even if they are unsure of whether they will use the technology. One paper reports that the preferred abbreviation for the library was already in use on Twitter when they went to establish an account (Cuddy, Graham, and Morton-Owens 2010). To help patrons find all sources of reference help, centralize all contact methods on one Ask Us/Ask a Librarian page, along with brief details of their best use. Don't forget to add in details for face-to-face services for those patrons seeking a more personalized reference encounter.

Use the tools to maximize their functionality—for example, quick posts on Twitter and slightly longer ones on Facebook, with links to a web page containing more information. Get to know the culture of the tool and work within this style of communication. As needed, adjust the content and style to meet user needs and to most effectively get the message out to patrons. Although there are easy ways to share information across multiple platforms (Twitter, Facebook, blogs) without modification, use this judiciously as too much repetition of the exact same content can be annoying to users who use multiple social media tools for library updates (DeVoe 2009, Tagtmeier 2010). Remember that different tools have varying definitions of *frequent* and *regular*. It is helpful to preschedule posts, tweets, and other updates when possible to avoid delays and ensure the regularity of new content, as well as having a roster of who is responsible for the updates. The overarching goal is provide information that is relevant to the reader in a form that they can use, which requires knowing both the culture of the tool and the needs of our patrons.

Social media tools, if used effectively, allow us to anticipate user questions, respond to complaints, accumulate compliments, and increase library goodwill by reaching out and being proactive. Several authors emphasize the value in monitoring student activity in social media forums and providing relevant information to them based on search results (Evans 2011, Forrestal 2011). For example, if tweets show an assignment deadline, post helpful tips on all tools and relevant web pages. The share tools in social media make it easy for readers to pass the information along to others. We cannot accurately quantify the effect of the sharing technology, but given the social nature of most patrons, it is very likely that a single useful post about an assignment would be shared with the majority of the students in the class.

Reference librarians should respond to the majority of comments and mentions in order to build rapport and community with patrons (Dickson and Holley 2010). This is similar to responding to comments and suggestions received through print means, e-mail, or online forms. Today's reference librarian needs to provide reference help through user-centered help objects and social media technologies, as well as being ready to synchronously or asynchronously provide high-quality responses to patron questions. Using tools discussed in this book and tips for their implementation, libraries can enhance their virtual reference offering and obtain increased user satisfaction.

REFERENCES

Abels, Eileen, and Malissa Ruffner. 2006. "Training for Online Virtual Reference: Measuring Effective Techniques." In *The Virtual Reference Desk: Creating a Reference Future.* Edited by David R Lankes, Eileen G. Abels, Marilyn Domas White, and Saira N. Haque, 49–73. New York: Neal-Schuman.

Ancelet, Lisa, Lorin Fisher, and Tara Spies. 2009. "Translating an Academic Library into Second Life." *Texas Library Journal* 85, no. 2: 52–55.

Blonde, Joe. 2006. "Staffing for Live Electronic Reference: Balancing Service and Sacrifice." In *The Virtual Reference Desk: Creating a Reference Future.* Edited by David R Lankes, Eileen G. Abels, Marilyn Domas White, and Saira N. Haque. 75–88. New York: Neal-Schuman Publishers.

Booth, Char. 2008. "Developing Skype-based Reference Services." *Internet Reference Quarterly* 13, no. 2/3: 147–165.

Cheney, Mari. 2010. "No Budget? No time? No Problem?" *AALL Spectrum* 15, no. 2: 28–30. www.aallnet.org/main-menu/Publications/spectrum/Archives/Vol-15/No-2/pub-sp1011-Virtual.pdf.

Cuddy, Colleen, Jamie Graham, and Emily G. Morton-Owens. 2010. "Implementing Twitter in a Health Sciences Library." *Medical Reference Services Quarterly* 29, no. 4: 320–330.

Dalson, Theresa, and Michael Pullin. 2008. "Virtual Reference on a Budget: Case Studies." *Library Media Connection* 27, no. 2: 30–33.

DeVoe, Kristina. 2009. "Constructing Who We Are Online: One Word, One Friend at a Time." *The Reference Librarian* 50, no. 4: 419–421.

Dickson, Andrea, and Robert P. Holley. 2010. "Social Networking in Academic Libraries: The Possibilities and the Concerns." *New Library World* 111, 11/12: 468–479.

Dumas, Eileen, and Victoria Peterson. 2010. "Second Life and Its Implications for Virtual Reference: Colorado and Beyond." *Colorado Libraries* 35, no. 1. http://coloradolibrariesjournal.org/node/32

Evans, Gwen. 2011. "LibAnswers." *The Charleston Advisor*, 12, no.4: 42–45.

Evans, Lorrie, Nina McHale, and Karen Sobel. 2009. "LibraryH3lp." *The Charleston Advisor* 10, no. 4: 25–29.

27

Fontichiaro, Kristin. 2008. "How Do I Love Skype? Let Me Count the Ways." *School Library Media Activities Monthly* 24, no. 7: 24–25.

Ford, Charlotte E., Julie Gerardin, Michelle Yamamoto, and Kelly Gordon. 2008. "Fresh Perspectives on Reference Work in Second Life." *Reference and User Services Quarterly* 47, no. 4: 324–330.

Forrestal, Valerie. 2011. "Making Twitter Work: A Guide for the Uninitiated, the Skeptical, and the Pragmatic." *The Reference Librarian* 52, no. 1/2: 146–151.

Gervasio, Darcy, Virginia Bryan, Emilie Steinmann. 2010. "Skype-Based Reference: A Study and Pilot Project." Presentation at the Wisconsin Library Association Annual Conference, Wisconsin Dells, Wisconsin. November 4.

Grabowska, Kasia. 2010. "Social Media Best Practices for Libraries: A TTW Guest Post." *Tame the Web* (blog). March 18. http://tametheweb.com/2010/03/18/social-media-best -practices-for-libraries/

Greene, Colleen. 2011. "Integrating Your LibraryH3lp Chat Widget in the New Facebook iFrame Tabs for Pages." *Colleen's Commentary* (blog). February 18. http:// colleenscommentary.net/2011/02/18/integrating-your-libraryh3lp-chat-widget-in-the -new-facebook-iframe-tabs-for-pages/.

Guder, Christopher. 2009. "Second Life as Innovation." Public Services Quarterly 5, no. 4: 282–288.

Hricko, Mary. 2010. "Using Microblogging Tools for Library Services." *Journal of Library Administration* 50, no. 4/6: 684–692.

Kern, M. Kathleen. 2009. *Virtual Reference Best Practices: Tailoring Services to Your Library*. Chicago: American Library Association.

Li, Lisa, and J. B. Hill. 2011. "Instant Assistance: The Use of LibraryH3lp at UALR." *Arkansas Libraries* 68, no. 2: 10–14.

Marstellar, Matthew, and Susan A Ware. 2006. "Models for Measuring and Evaluating Reference Costs." *Library Research and Publications.* Paper 68. http://repository.cmu .edu/lib_science/68.

Meola, Mark, and Sam Stormont. 2002. *Starting and Operating Live Virtual Reference Services*. New York: Neal-Schuman.

Ronan, Jana Smith. 2003. *Chat Reference: A Guide to Live Virtual Reference Services*. Westport, CT: Libraries Unlimited.

Sachs, Dianna E., Edward J. Eckel, and Kathleen A. Langan. 2011. "Striking a Balance: Effective Use of Facebook in an Academic Library." *Internet Reference Services Quarterly* 16, no. 1/2: 35–54.

Segerstrom, Jan. 2007. "Can U Skype Me Be 4 Noon?" *Information Searcher* 17, no 4:1–7.

Sekyere, Kwabena. 2009. "Too Much Hullabaloo about Facebook in Libraries! Is It Really Helping Libraries?" *Nebraska Library Association Quarterly* 40, no. 2: 22–27.

Sessoms, Pam, and Eric Sessoms. 2008. "LibraryH3lp: A New Flexible Chat Reference System." *Code{4}lib Journal* 4. http://journal.code4lib.org/articles/107.

Steiner, Heidi. 2009. "Reference Utility of Social Networking Sites: Options and Functionality." *Library Hi Tech News* 26, 5/6: 4–6.

Strothmann, Molly, Cheryl McCain, and Laurie Scrivener. 2009. "Ask A Librarian' Pages as Reference Gateways to Academic Libraries." *The Reference Librarian* 50, no 3: 259–275.

Sutton, Paul. July 6, 2010. "10 Reasons You're Not Getting Followers on Twitter." *Social Media Today* (blog). July 6. http://socialmediatoday.com/thepaulsutton/142832/10 -reasons-you%E2%80%99re-not-getting-followers-twitter.

Tagtmeier, Curt. 2010. "Facebook vs Twitter: Battle of the Social Network Stars." *Computers in Libraries* 30, no. 7: 7–10. http://www.infotoday.com/cilmag/sep10/ Tagtmeier.shtml

Tang, Florence. 2010. "Reference Tools in Second Life: Implications for Real Life Libraries." *New Library World* 111, no. 11/12: 513–525.

Theiss-White, Danielle, Jenny Dale, Melia Erin Fritch, Laura Bonella, and Jason Coleman. 2009. "IM'ing Overload: LibraryH3lp to the Rescue." *Library Hi Tech News* 26, no. 1/2: 12–17.

Weimer, Keith. 2010. "Text Messaging the Reference Desk: Using Upside Wireless' SMS-to-E-mail to Extend Reference Service." *The Reference Librarian* 51, no. 2: 108–123.

Welch, Jeanie M. 2005a. "The Electronic Welcome Mat: The Academic Library Web Site as a Marketing and Public Relations Tool." *Journal of Academic Librarianship* 31(3): 225-228.

Welch, Jeanie M. 2005b. "Who Says We're Not Busy? Library Web Page Usage as a Measure of Public Service Activity." *Reference Services Review* 33(4): 371–379.

Young, Jeff. 2010. "Researchers Find 'Million-Follower Fallacy' in Twitter." *Wired Campus Blog. The Chronicle of Higher Education*, May 25. http://chronicle.com/blogs/ wiredcampus/researchers-find-million-follower-fallacy-in- twitter/24290.

Using Twitter for Virtual Reference Services

Ellen Hampton Filgo

Twitter launched in 2006, taking the Web 2.0 world by storm and quickly growing into one of its hottest commodities. Initially, Twitter asked people "What are you doing?" which has morphed into "What's happening?" and gave them 140 characters in which to answer Twitter's opening screen. With updates from the Web, via SMS and now from a variety of mobile and web applications, Twitter helps people quickly update their followers as to their moment-to-moment activities and to join Twitter's distributed conversations. Today, everyone from businesses, world leaders, reporters, celebrities, athletes—and perhaps even your families, friends and neighbors—have established a Twitter presence, realizing the importance of this easy-to-use microblogging service in interacting with friends, customers, patrons, and strangers in order get their voices heard or establish their brands. Twitter now claims over 100 million active users (Twitter 2011).

Libraries, too, have joined the Twitter phenomenon, some even quite early on. A 2007 *Library Technology Report* highlighted several libraries for the creative ways they provided information to their patrons: by tweeting recent reference questions, library news, and events; or by feeding existing library RSS feeds from blogs or recently cataloged items into the Twitter stream (Stephens 2007). However, early library experiments with Twitter were focused primarily on different ways to broadcast information in a one-way, library-to-patron model, rather than as a way to interact or converse with patrons. This is understandable, for in the early days when Twitter was not as well-known, library patrons wouldn't have necessarily been using the service. Having a library Twitter account was just an easy way for librarians to update people about news and events, and the Twitter API and numerous third-party applications made it easy to embed library Tweets on a blog or other web page. Patrons did not need a Twitter account to see the updates.

While a how-to article on Twitter for libraries in 2009 indicates that "conversational Twittering is not yet the norm among libraries" (Milstein 2009, 18), library patrons on Twitter today expect to be able to interact with the institutions and organizations they follow, and libraries ought to take note. There still may be some libraries who determine that a policy to not follow users is the best for their institution (Starr 2010, 24); however, in order to best utilize Twitter for virtual reference services, finding and following users, monitoring questions and comments, and connecting with patrons in conversation are vital.

SETTING UP TWITTER FOR REFERENCE

Account Creation

Setting up a Twitter account for your library is easy. You only need a name, an e-mail, and a password to get started. You can then choose a username depending upon availability. For best results, make sure that your account has an avatar that reflects your library (whether it is a logo, a picture of the library building, or smiling librarian faces) and that you also customize your account's background with any other pictures, logos, or marketing information. In your account settings, fill out the "bio" and "URL" fields with pertinent information and the website address for your library. Figure 2.1 shows an example of the personal account page; figure 2.2. provides an example of the account settings page.

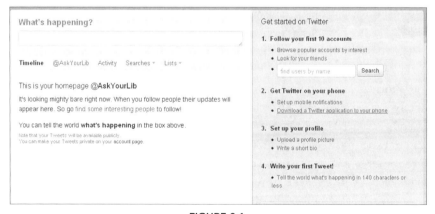

FIGURE 2.1
Twitter Personal Account Home Page

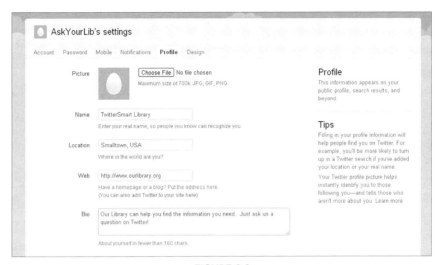

FIGURE 2.2
Twitter Personal Account Settings Page

33

Staffing

Choosing who will post to the Twitter account and monitor incoming questions is an important decision. In some cases, perhaps it was an enterprising emerging tech-oriented librarian who originally set up the library Twitter account. In other cases, perhaps a feasibility committee had to be formed to discuss whether Twitter is the right service for your library to offer. In either case, the question of who will be responsible for updating and monitoring it is an important key to a successful service. Who will staff it—reference librarians? Systems or web services librarians? The library director? Library marketing and communications staff? Some combination? Obviously this depends on which staff members at your library are willing and available to monitor the service and knowledgeable to answer any questions or concerns. Whatever the decision on your library's part, the recommendation is that it be staffed by a team who is responsible for regular updates and monitoring for questions or comments. If your library is small and too short-staffed to create a team, make sure the person in charge has been given time and flexibility to accommodate this responsibility.

Finding Followers

For your Twitter account to have any impact, it needs followers. Beyond the obvious desire for your library to have users to receive messages, followers are an important part of the infrastructure of Twitter. Followers allow you to have meaningful conversations about your library materials, services, and policies. By using the @reply function in Twitter, your followers can ask the library questions, as well as alert their own followers to the fact that your library is on Twitter, as shown in figure 2.3. Followers can also extend the reach of your Twitter account by retweeting interesting pieces of information to their own followers.

Marketing your Twitter account is essential to increase your number of followers. Ensure that your library's Twitter account is regularly and actively updated. Your Twitter marketing campaign, whether it's a simple link from your library's web page or a viral marketing blitz with multimedia messaging, may drive people to your site, but having interesting and helpful information and regular interaction with patrons will keep them coming back. There might be some curious patrons who follow your Twitter account on their own initiative as well. However, the best way to increase your following is to actively find and follow people yourself. Twitter users are aware that their accounts are open to the world, and they also have the

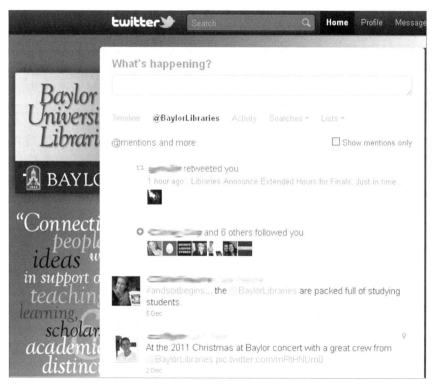

FIGURE 2.3
Twitter Mentions

option to lock them down. Following local users, university students or professors and library patrons is the quickest way to let active Twitter users know that your account exists.

You can use the Twitter search function to find people who mention your library (fig. 2.4). The next section provides tips on searching effectively. While it would be easy to simply follow every user who follows your library account, be careful about adding followers without checking on their validity. There are many spam

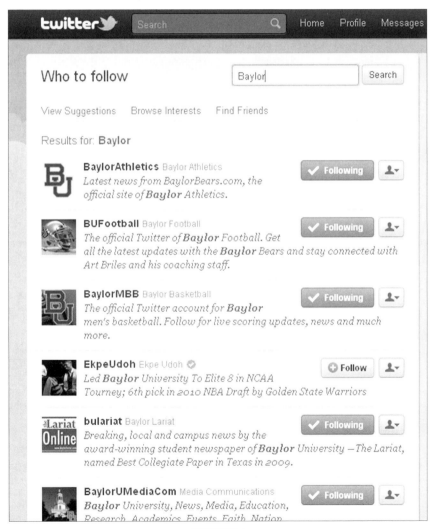

FIGURE 2.4
Twitter Search Results Page

accounts, or accounts that exist solely to promote questionable or pornographic material. Often these accounts will auto follow a large number of users at once. You shouldn't automatically follow back anyone that follows your account. The easiest way to find your patrons is to use a search application such as the ones listed here:

Twitter.com's "Who to Follow" service (http://twitter.com/#!/who_to_follow) suggests similar users to the ones that you have recently followed. One result for "Baylor" is shown in figure 2.5.

WeFollow.com is one of the biggest Twitter directories out there. You can add your library's account in up to five hashtag groupings, as well as your town. Then you can use the groupings to search for like-minded users or patrons.

Twellow.com is considered a "Twitter Yellow Pages." You can use this site to search for local users or patrons who have listed your town, university, or college in their bio field and have added themselves to the Twellow .com directory.

Tweetfind.com searches for your keywords or terms in Twitter account bios and recent tweets. One good feature is that it also searches through

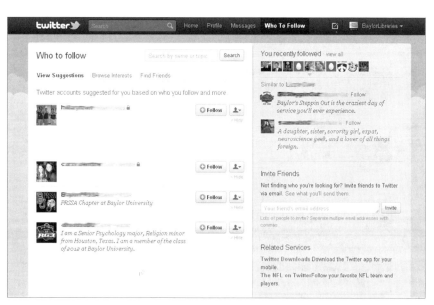

FIGURE 2.5
Who to Follow Search Result

Twitter lists to find related users. However, unlike some other directories, you have to log in with your Twitter account to even do a simple search.

Locafollow.com can search by keyword through the Twitter bios, locations, names and tweets. Powered by Google Search, it retrieves only what Google indexes, not what Twitter provides. It's also limited by Google's search API and thus can only retrieve sixty-four results for any one search.

MONITORING TWITTER REFERENCE

Monitoring by Searches, RSS, and #hashtags

Twitter's integrated search function (http://search.twitter.com) can be a great place to find other Twitter users who are mentioning your library. The advanced search operators can help you narrow down and target local Twitter users and patrons.

Here are a few tips for monitoring your local Twitter stream:

1. Search @yourusername to find mentions. Your Twitter profile page provides an easy reference to these tweets.
2. Search Twitter using relevant keywords: library, study, book, research, cite. Be creative! What does your community of users or patrons talk about? If there are a number of libraries in your local area and "library" is too generic a keyword, try your library name.
3. Use the *near:* operator with your town or zip code to narrow down your results to your local area. Use the *within:* operator to narrow or broaden the area around the town or zip code.

There are also a few third-party Twitter applications that allow for location-based searching. Some examples are:

GeoChirp.com. You can search this Google map mashup for a location to see tweets from that location and search for keywords within the results. *Pros:* automatically detects your location; allows an RSS feed of your search; lists top Twitter accounts in your area; can log in with your Twitter account to automatically respond to and retweet other accounts. *Cons:* not many—it is a very well-developed and effective application.

ChirpCity.com. Limit your search down to a state or city and it will display both Tweets *from* that location as well as *about* that location. *Pros:*

different angle on searching for a location. *Cons:* no way to search within your results for specific keywords.

NearbyTweets.com. Add your location and some keywords to load a real-time updating list of tweets from a particular area. *Pros:* real-time updating. *Cons:* cannot seem to detect location, so it must be changed manually; changing keywords tends to bog the site down.

Hashtags, such as #ala2011, are a good way to track certain subjects. Conferences, events, organizations, affiliated groups of people as well as user-generated jokes and memes all use hashtags to aggregate like-minded content. Hashtags can be acronyms, words, or phrases proceeded by the # symbol. Search through your followers to see if they are using any local hashtags. Perhaps there is one related to your town or your university. If not, why not create one? Start using it with appropriate content and hopefully it will catch on! An example of a Twitter post showing the use of multiple hashtags is shown in figure 2.6.

3:30 AM and #clubmoody is still pretty packed. #itsthattimeoftheyear #finals #hellweek

5 Dec via Twitter for iPhone ☆ Favorite ⇄ Retweet ↩ Reply

FIGURE 2.6
Twitter Post with Multiple Hashtags

LibraryH3lp

Since LibraryH3lp (http://libraryh3lp.com) was launched in 2008, it has become a very popular virtual reference service among many different types of libraries, from small public libraries to larger university libraries to statewide virtual reference consortia. The LibraryH3lp platform has proven to be very adaptable to new virtual reference services, including using both Google Voice and Twilio for text-a-librarian services. In January 2010, LibraryH3lp introduced a gateway for Twitter accounts (Sessoms, 2010). Setting up this gateway allows for any Twitter status updates that begin with an @-mention of your library's Twitter account to be directed to the staff monitoring the LibraryH3lp virtual reference service. The answer is routed back through Twitter.

LibAnswers

Springshare, the creator of the popular LibGuides subject guide and content management software, launched LibAnswers (http://springshare.com/libanswers/) in April 2009. LibAnswers is an ask-a-librarian service with a built-in public FAQ and staff knowledge base. If a library using LibAnswers sets up Twitter integration, any question asked on Twitter and directed @ your library's account will be directed into the LibAnswers dashboard for answering, along with questions asked through the web interface or SMS. Then within the LibAnswers dashboard, the librarian can tweet back to the patron that their question has been answered. Questions asked and answered via Twitter can be added to the library's knowledge base.

Mosio

Mosio, the creators of the popular Text a Librarian service, developed an app called Twitter Answers. Using this app, librarians can answer the questions of people who follow the Twitter account @qna and ask it questions. While this is a neat feature, your patrons do not directly ask your library questions, nor would your librarians who might answer questions know which questions are even from your patrons.

SUCCESS STORIES

Academic Library: Baylor University

The Baylor University Libraries has a team approach to staffing their Twitter account, @BaylorLibraries, which was begun in 2008. The home page for the Baylor account is shown in figure 2.7. Currently, there are four people with the password privileges and ability to update: two staff from the Marketing and Communication Department, the director of the Central Libraries, and the e-learning librarian in the Reference Department. There are a few special collections libraries on campus (for example, the Texas Collection, @texascollection, and the Armstrong Browning Library, @BrowningLibrary) that have separate Twitter accounts, and they have only one or two people responsible for updates. Ultimately, the Marketing and Communication (M&C) Department oversees social media initiatives for all the campus libraries.

Most of the news and events that publish to the Baylor Libraries' Twitter stream are automated via RSS feeds or Twitterfeed, and come from the published news on our website or a variety of library blogs. (See the sidebar for a list of helpful blogs.) Information about special events is posted by the M&C staff. These staff members, who have more time (and a mandate) to monitor social media, answer almost all of the questions that are directed to the library via @ mentions, and followed through TweetDeck or HootSuite. If there is a question or a complaint about specific policies, the appropriate administrative or reference librarians are

FIGURE 2.7

Twitter Page—Baylor University Libraries

consulted for an answer. The e-learning librarian also monitors certain keywords from local users through RSS feeds, which are checked regularly. Often, this librarian can find opinions, praise, or complaints about library services or policies that aren't specifically directed at the library's account and can answer them proactively. The e-learning librarian has also established a LibraryH3lp gateway for the Twitter account with a queue that sends the questions directly to her IM client. The librarian and the M&C staff also closely follow a few local hashtags: (#baylor, #baylorproud, and #bucampus), a few library created hashtags: (#baylorlib and #baylorits), as well as nicknames students have for certain areas of the library (#clubmoody and #clubjones).

While the majority of questions asked on the Baylor Libraries' Twitter account are not heavily research focused, this seems to follow the trend the Baylor reference librarians have seen in the types of virtual reference questions that come via other "quick" virtual reference mediums, such as SMS/text-a-librarian services. Twitter questions are mainly directional questions, policy questions, and technology help. Figures 2.8 shows a typical reference transaction.

Baylor Library Blogs Feeding Into Twitter Account

Baylor Libraries News
The RSS feed from our content management system's news feature.

Digital Collections of Baylor University
http://blogs.baylor.edu/digitalcollections/
The blog from the digitization group at the libraries.

Library411
http://blogs.baylor.edu/library411/
The blog of "Tips, Tricks and Tools to make your research better."

New Electronic Resources @ BU
http://blogs.baylor.edu/new_electronic_resources/
The blog that announces new acquisitions of electronic resources and databases.

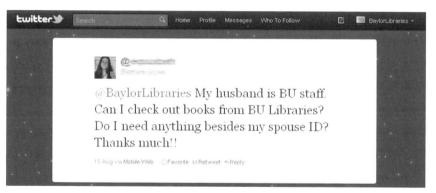

FIGURE 2.8
Twitter Reference Question and Response

Public Library: Cleveland Public Library

The Cleveland Public Library, @Cleveland_PL, has eagerly embraced Twitter as a tool for communication, and was even cited as a good example of a library embracing Twitter in a 2009 article (Milstein 2009). While the Cleveland Public Library (CPL) is a large metropolitan library system, their central marketing and communication department is not large; therefore they contract with a public relations firm to help with their Facebook and Twitter efforts. The firm knows the library's event schedule and is kept up-to-date with information about new resources and initiatives and posts tweets accordingly, using the HootSuite Twitter application. While the majority of the Twitter posting and monitoring is done by the PR firm, the web applications manager at the CPL also pays attention to Twitter activity and has access to post tweets and answer any questions, particularly if the PR firm is not able to answer a question. In those cases, the manager is notified by the firm of the Twitter question. The Cleveland Public Library is a good example of a library with limited staff to dedicate to Twitter and other social media by using a team approach, even if it is outsourced. Figure 2.9 shows the CPL Twitter page.

FIGURE 2.9
Twitter Page—Cleveland Public Library

The library receives a lot of questions from Twitter. An example of a question and answer is shown in figure 2.10. The web applications manager notes that these days, a lot of the tweeted questions have to do with e-books and e-book access questions (Pawlowski 2011) as well as questions about events and technology policies. The library is very interactive with its patrons, thanking them for mentions, retweets, and praise about library services. They also readily use hashtags, particularly local Cleveland initiatives, such as #CleveEvents and #HappyinCleve, as well as Twitter-wide hashtags like #FF or #FollowFriday (a weekly post noting which Twitter accounts are good to follow). Twitter can also handle more academic questions and answers, as shown in figure 2.11 taken from University of North Carolina's Davis Library Twitter feed.

FIGURE 2.10
Twitter Question to and Response from Cleveland Public Library

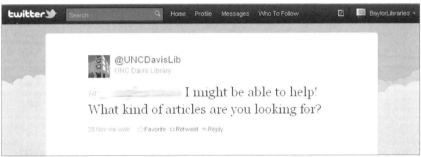

FIGURE 2.11
Reference Interview via Twitter

TWITTER NOW AND IN THE FUTURE

Twitter can be a fun and effective way to engage your patrons in virtual reference services. Using Twitter to its fullest potential—not just as an information broadcast, but as a conversational, back-and-forth medium—libraries can reach their patrons with answers to their questions. By actively monitoring the library's followers as well as mentions of the library and its services through searches and hashtags, libraries can be proactive in reaching out to patrons with help. Library patrons who use Twitter are familiar with its interactive conversational dynamic, and they respond well to the type of reference service that libraries offer through Twitter.

Twitter has developed in many ways since its initial launch. Some of those developments—the integration of the @ reply or RT (retweeting) into the basic functionality of the site—were taken directly from standards that Twitter users themselves had adopted. How Twitter will develop in the future is yet to be seen, but there is no doubt that it will continue to grow and change. Libraries, with our strong service- and patron-oriented attitudes, should strive to be active in the Twitter community, particularly for the chance to influence future changes.

45

REFERENCES

Milstein, Sarah. 2009. "Twitter for Libraries (and Librarians)." *Computers in Libraries* 29, no. 5: 17–18.

Pawlowski, Amy. 2011. Twitter at the CPL. Phone. September 14.

Schroeder, Stan. 2008. Mosio Uses Twitter For Mobile Q&A. *Mashable* (blog). January 30. http://mashable.com/2008/01/30/mosio-uses-twitter-for-mobile-qa/.

Sessoms, Pam. 2010. "New Gateways: Twitter and Google Talk via Google Apps." *LibraryH3lp*. January 18. http://libraryh3lp.blogspot.com/2010/01/new-gateways -twitter-and-google-talk.html.

Starr, Joan. 2010. "California Digital Library in Twitter-Land." *Computers in Libraries* 30, no. 7: 23–27.

Stephens, Michael. 2007. "Messaging in a 2.0 World." *Library Technology Reports* 43, no. 5: 2–66.

Twitter. 2011. "One Hundred Million Voices." *Twitter Blog*. September 8. http://blog .twitter.com/2011/09/one-hundred-million-voices.html.

Using Google Voice and Chat for Reference at the Kelvin Smith Library

Brian C. Gray

The Kelvin Smith Library (KSL), the main library at Case Western Reserve University (CWRU) in Cleveland, Ohio, has provided virtual reference services for many years to just under ten thousand students, approximately six thousand employees, over one hundred thousand alumni, and others seeking information. The virtual reference services are supported by thirteen people, including librarians, library assistants, and one graduate student. Hours of virtual offerings match the physical desk operations and total 72.5 hours per week during an academic semester. Some virtual services are staffed by the same person managing the physical desk, while others are staffed by a second person during each assigned shift.

The library's in-person reference transactions account for 55 percent of all interactions, but virtual reference interactions are climbing over time. E-mail (17 percent), instant messaging (6 percent), and embedded chat (5 percent) are integral tools in reference and outreach services. The embedded chat is a service contract through LivePerson (www.liveperson.com) and staffed by the library's reference staff. It can be found throughout the library's website and many of the available research databases.

GOING TO GOOGLE

A change in service philosophy and user preferences required a change in how virtual references services were offered. The university switched many communication and productivity tools to Google Apps, so users were becoming comfortable with Google e-mail and chat. Instant messaging (IM) usage has continued to drop from services not related to Google, and IM does not resonant well with the newer generations of students. Library staff has been told that instant messaging has been replaced by text messaging and Facebook. Smartphone usage and text messaging continue to grow among the library's users. In addition, as staff continues to gain more instruction responsibilities, reference tasks need to be streamlined.

The KSL had specific requirements when establishing its new text messaging reference service. As this was a considered a pilot attempt to judge user acceptance and capabilities, the service needed be implemented with no additional funding for software, staffing, or training. It needed to be quick to set up and train staff, as the official announcement was to be made a couple weeks later in preparation for an already planned open house. The library had implemented a new internal mindset of practicing nimble and agile exploration, and the text messaging pilot allowed the staff to explore that new process. Finally, services were explored with the hope to simplify and homogenize most or all virtual offerings into a cohesive service point. Librarians were required to be familiar with many virtual communications tools (e-mail, instant messaging, and chat). The triage of e-mail messages required several steps for each e-mail as a single person forwarded them to the appropriate expert. The hope was that with a new interface for e-mails through a Google account and the addition of Google Voice tools, the plethora of offerings would be easier to manage.

ESTABLISHING A GOOGLE VOICE ACCOUNT

Google Voice (www.google.com/voice/) offers many advantages in offering phone and text messaging reference services to users. Some of the highlights of the free service include online voice mail, voice-mail transcription, text messaging in the Gmail interface, and other customizations. The system provides a single private phone number for calls and text messages. The library has decided other competing text messaging services were not as user friendly because they were based in a shared phone number with other organizations. The services with a shared number required advertising an organization-specific, several-digit code that forced the text message to be routed to the proper organization. The end user thus needed to remember a phone number and special code to communicate. Google Voice does not have this requirement.

Google Voice account creation is a simple process of completing an online application. Information required includes your current e-mail address, password, location, birthday, word verification (to avoid computer automated creation of accounts), and agreement to the terms of service. A verification e-mail will be sent to your current e-mail account to complete the process. If you do not have a Google account, use another e-mail address for your log-in address. If you already have a Google account, you can sign in to add Google Voice to your existing account.

The finalization of a Google Voice account is a fairly simple process. At your first log-in or when you continue from the link in the verification e-mail, you can request a Google Voice phone number. You can also link the account to an existing mobile number if desired. Phone numbers can be chosen by entering the zip code of your target audience or a specific word, phrase, or number. One advantage of picking by zip code is you could establish a local phone number if you have a distant user group outside the locality of your traditional phone service. Word choice can allow you to integrate with current branding or make for an easy-to-remember phone number. You will also be asked for a four-digit personal identification number to access the included voice mail. Finally, you will be asked if you want to forward your Google Voice number to an existing phone number. Kelvin Smith Library has forwarded Google calls to the phone at the physical reference desk. You will need to receive a confirmation phone call at the existing phone number so you can enter a code given to you by Google during the installation. This one-time confirmation phone call gives you your first opportunity to record your incoming voice-mail welcome message. You can add multiple forwarding phone numbers so all specified phones ring whenever someone calls this single Google Voice phone number, thus the call will definitely be answered. Figure 3.1 shows the location of the Google Voice service on the ASK Kelvin Smith Library page.

The Google Voice interface, shown in figure 3.2, is simple to use and requires little training. Voice mail can be listened to using a computer's sound capabilities. If a microphone is available, a return call can be initiated with a simple click, or alternatively Google will call your forwarded physical phone and the library patron simultaneously. Other power features that benefit a group of people sharing a single account, such as a library's reference department, include the ability to add notes, e-mail the voice mail, block a caller, or download the audio file for every call or message in the account. The account owner can also get the html code to embed the voice mail in a website or other application such as a FAQ or an internal training sheet. A text message can be sent to the caller with a single click, and Google counts the characters to help keep the message short. The interface organizes calls into the categories voice mail, text, place, received, and missed for easy statistics

FIGURE 3.1
ASK Kelvin Smith Library Home Page

recording. A built-in contacts list simplifies organization of important contact information. Voice mail is transcribed to text for convenience, so you can prepare a response before even listening to the voice mail. The library staff likes this feature in supporting privacy of phone calls while working in the public areas.

Google Voice supports various methods of operation, which allows libraries to customize the service to their needs. Google provides support to integrate the voice service with an existing mobile phone, although the main advantage in KSL's usage of Google Voice is that a mobile phone is not needed. The account owner can call Google using their registered physical phone to record voice-mail greetings and other custom audio messages, so a computer-based microphone is not necessary. Text messages can be forwarded to an e-mail account; and if Gmail is used, they can be answered from that e-mail account. Google Voices lets you set up Caller ID features so the caller must say their name before proceeding with their question.

FIGURE 3.2
Google Voice Librarian Screen

A "do not disturb" feature allows missed calls to be e-mailed to an account of your choice. The Group setting lets you create lists of friends, family, and coworkers, so that when a particular person calls, a custom experience can take place; the caller hears a specific greeting, for example, or is put through to a particular reference librarian's extension. Another exciting feature is to embed a call widget in a website that lets your users initiate a phone call by clicking on a logo embedded in your website. Users do not need to have an audio capable computer to use the widget; after they provide their phone number, Google calls you and them simultaneously.

EXTRA ADVANTAGE:
E-MAIL MANAGEMENT AND GOOGLE CHAT

Google's e-mail service, called Gmail, allowed the KSL's Reference Department to simplify the management of various e-mail addresses. Previously, an alias was set up on the university's Sympa (www.sympa.org) e-mail list manager service, which allowed communications to be forwarded to the primary contact and two backup people. The person previewed the e-mails and distributed them to other library staff to answer from a personal work e-mail account. The two major disadvantages of this system were the time needed to triage the message and the delay the process took before the actual expert received the message. The system also required each individual to report transaction statistics at various points throughout the calendar year. Some organizations do have a shared e-mail account to answer questions. One person is usually assigned to monitor the queue and respond to questions or triage to other experts. The blending of Google services moved the KSL's processes toward a similar approach while adding the new voice services.

Through taking advantage of all the Google offerings, e-mail and virtual reference services were simplified. It was decided that the Reference Department would use Google Voice, Gmail, and Google Chat for virtual interactions. All variations of current and past reference e-mail addresses were forwarded to the single Gmail account, so no communications were lost and no single individual's e-mail account was filled with content. Google Gmail settings could be configured so the library patron sees an e-mail address that matches the university domain, such as asksl@case.edu. The person assigned to the physical reference desk is delegated to distribute e-mails to other staff. E-mails are now processed in less than twenty-four hours, which was not happening with the previous triage method.

To best use the Gmail interface for all e-mail, Google chat, and text messaging interactions, we found that some customization streamlined the process. Google Voice was set to display voice mail and text messages in the same inbox as all the regular e-mail messages. On the top right of each Google interface screen, there is an image of a gear that will allow settings to be changed for that specific interface or service. In the voice-mail setting, under "Voicemail & Text," the library selected the option to have all voice mail and text messages sent to the Gmail account. Due to the setting selected, Google E-mail was now used as the default interface for daily interactions. Now, one staff member can manage all virtual communications

The Value of Using Gmail Labels and Archives

- You can identify messages by type of question, length of question, department or librarian responsible, or any other categories that are needed

- You can identify and sort e-mails by category

- Using archive folders, you can store e-mails within categories

- You can keep e-mail inbox and archives organized for effective communications from any Internet accessible computer. Trillian (www.trillian.im) can be used to monitor the Gmail account (or other e-mail) where texts are being sent. This will help reduce the lag time between someone sending a text and the staff knowing about it, especially if staff members are multitasking. Boeninger (2010) provides a helpful guide to setting up a Google Voice account and linking it to Trillian.

Statistics collection, assessment of results, and training of new reference staff was simplified by using Gmail's label and archive functions at the end of the process. After each e-mail, text message, or voice mail is answered or assigned to an individual, the staff member labels it with the last name of the person who answered it or to whom the message was forwarded. Labels were created such as "Text Messages" or other special transactions that needed to be tracked, such as a contest that was conducted. The message is also archived so it no longer appears in the in-box. The advantage of this process includes being able to keep statistics for each person, knowing all questions were answered, and keeping a history of the interactions if the patron follows up later. It also creates an internal repository of communications to be used for assessment of the service or training new staff.

SUCCESS WITH GOOGLE VOICE AND APPS

Since the implementation in fall 2010, the results were strong. Staff found no difficulties in using the Google tools, and work was now equally distributed among everyone. In slightly more than one year of usage, one thousand e-mails were answered and organized among thirty labels for easy recall at a later date. Text messaging operated as a pilot for the first year with minimal advertising, but eighty messages were replied to it. In the future, a full marketing campaign will be developed in promotion of text messaging reference. One extra advantage to using Google Voice is the interest in providing open source help. For example, there is now a Google Voice Quick Reference Card available (Cool Geex 2010).

LESSONS LEARNED AND FUTURE PLANS

The library staff has found Google Voice—and the related Gmail and chat—to be very easy to implement and manage. Staff had some early trouble adapting to the tools as Google products seem to be in consistent beta mode. It means the products are always improving but change is fairly regular. Staff did not find the

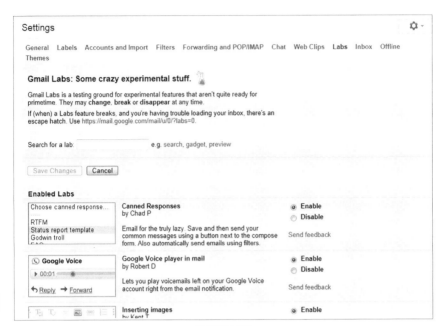

FIGURE 3.3
Google Labs Interface

changes hard to manage, although it was a mindset change in comparison to the tools used previously. Staff also tried various combinations of Google Labs features, which can be found from the settings screen with the Gmail interface, as shown in figure 3.3. The challenge was remembering that any changes affected all users of the account. However, the system was eventually configured to meet most of the staff requirements.

Several future projects are being considered as they relate to the library's virtual reference tool kit. A pilot project will be conducted in the near future to explore the audio/video chat functionality of the existing Google Chat. The KSL staff wants to explore which transactions would benefit from video chat, and if library staff visibility during transaction can be used to promote the people of the library or make the transaction more comfortable to the patron. Phasing out of other instant messaging offerings, such as Yahoo! is being considered because the university is a Google campus. Finally, the library will phase out the university-provided phone number for the Reference Desk, as the Circulation Desk will be first contact for library patrons. Librarians will be available by appointment via the shared Google phone number or other virtual communication offerings. The KSL staff has enjoyed providing assistance through the integrated tool set by levering Google's capabilities.

REFERENCES

Boeninger, Chad. 2010. "Implementing a Text Reference Service on the Cheap." *LibraryVoice* (blog), October 14. http://libraryvoice.com/technology/text-reference-for-free.

Cool Geex.2010. "Google Voice Quick Reference Card 2.0." *Coolgeex* (blog), February 2. http://www.coolgeex.com/google-voice-quick-reference-guide-v2-0/.

Virtual Reference at UNLV Libraries
From Infancy to Popular Student Service

Sidney Lowe and Darcy Del Bosque

HISTORY OF CHAT REFERENCE AT THE UNLV LIBRARIES

Chat reference has been an evolving service at the University of Nevada–Las Vegas Libraries since it was first envisioned in the early 2000s. Formal and informal assessment paired with staff and patron needs led to incremental changes that have totally transformed the service over the last decade. By remaining responsive to user and library needs, we've been able to expand the service while not straining diminishing library resources.

The university libraries began to explore the possibility of a chat reference service in 2002. We were looking for a multifunctional system that would provide the best services to our library patrons and one that staff could easily adapt to and be trained to use. The UNLV Libraries ventured into virtual reference services in early 2004, with a subscription to OCLC's QuestionPoint (www.questionpoint .org). This software package allowed us to manage e-mail reference questions, to transfer queries between librarians, and to track usage. At that time, a collaborative agreement for managing reference questions 24/7 was a function we thought would be a great help to our users, since we did not have the staff or budget to support around-the-clock access on our own.

Unfortunately, we had difficulties not only with the shared reference service, but also with the co-browsing feature of QuestionPoint, which was not consistent or reliable. We became dissatisfied with the program when we realized it had become cumbersome for both library users and for librarians, and many times it simply did not function well. Most of the problems were with the chat feature. Users would unexpectedly be disconnected and became frustrated, and at times, library staff members were suddenly booted out of the system without warning. UNLV Libraries staff became discouraged with the limitations, poor performance, and cost-to-benefit ratio of the QuestionPoint service. After many attempts at problem solving between customer and vendor, we were unable to resolve these and other difficulties with the system. An administrative decision was made to cancel our subscription after investigating other virtual reference options. In spring 2005, the libraries switched to providing chat reference through instant messaging (IM).

There were several reasons this looked like a viable and promising service for UNLV Libraries:

- Many students were familiar with and already using this technology.
- There was no cost.
- Setting up the system was not difficult.
- It worked fairly easily.
- It had a clean interface.
- Subject pages and librarians could have their own unique IM by simply creating an appropriate and different screen name for the specific purpose. Virtual reference software cost at the time was approximately $3,000 per librarian.
- User privacy was better protected. There were privacy concerns regarding the retention of virtual reference system transcripts for three to four months with no local control over this decision.

However, there were some disadvantages with IM:

- No "bells and whistles" such as pushing web pages or co-browsing, although staff and users could send URLs.
- E-mail questions were no longer easily managed.
- We lost the built-in statistics tracking.
- We were on our own; no longer part of a shared responsibility network.
- We could not transfer chats from one librarian to another.
- We had log-in problems, including knowing when to log in, as there was no built-in scheduling function.
- Scripts were not automatically stored; staff had to copy and paste an entire conversation if it needed to be archived.

A big concern was the loss of the built-in statistics tracking, so we asked our Web and Digital Services Department to build a statistics database with web front-end data entry. It was called the IM Statistics Generator, which worked well for a while, but it was incumbent upon each "chatter" on the staff to remember to log their transaction.

Initially instant messaging was staffed using the free program Trillian (www .trillian.im), which was installed on the computers of all of the chat service providers. This program allowed staff to monitor instant messaging traffic from different service providers—in our case AIM, Yahoo! Messenger, and MSN Messenger. Individual librarian accounts were created for handing off the service, since only one person could be logged in at a time. The person taking over would log on to their personal account, message the person currently staffing the service, and ask if it they were ready for them to log on. This prevented someone being unintentionally disconnected during a chat. As new technologies became available, some staff members switched from using Trillian to a service called Meebo (www .meebo.com). Meebo was also free but ran online, so no software program had to be installed. This allowed people to staff chat away from their office computers.

Although the transition from QuestionPoint to instant messaging was an improvement, there were still challenges with the system. Patrons needed to have their own instant messaging account, be logged into it, and be friends with the account unlvlibraries in order to use the service. Library staff had to monitor several instant messaging clients at one time, and only one librarian could be logged in to chat at a time. Statistics and transcripts were not automatically recorded, requiring extra steps for staff to track sessions.

LIBRARYH3LP

As new technologies emerged, librarians continued to evaluate them to see if there were alternatives that could eliminate these challenges. Initially Meebo was eyed as a possible way to enhance the instant messaging service because it allowed all accounts to be monitored through one entry point, it provided the ability to create chat widgets, and many staff were already using it. However, after investigation, a library-specific service called LibraryH3lp (libraryh3lp.com) became the primary suggestion for an upgraded chat service.

LibraryH3lp is a platform for instant messaging that was created specifically for libraries. Like the instant messaging service that was currently in place, Library

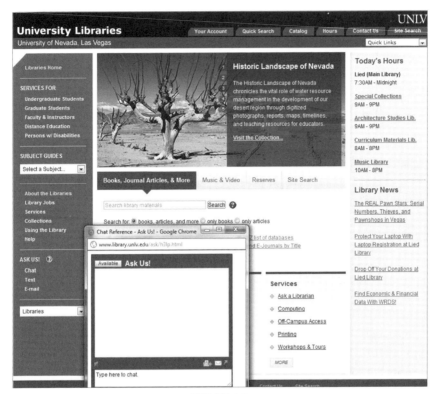

FIGURE 4.1
UNLV Libraries Chat Widget

H3lp allows staffing several IM services (AOL, Google Talk, Yahoo!, Hotmail) at one time. It includes a chat widget feature so patrons do not need to sign into their own IM accounts to get help, but can simply type into a box on a web page, as shown in figure 4.1. The system also allows multiple library staff to be logged into the service at one time and transfer questions between one another as needed. A nice side benefit to multiple simultaneous log-ins is that it helped to fill vacancies in the chat reference schedule because several staff started logging in to chat as a daily routine. Frequently staff members are standing by to answer chat questions even when there is no one officially scheduled for chat during a given hour.

Additionally, LibraryH3lp can create multiple queues so different chat services can be created and staffed by different groups of people, as shown in figure 4.2. This model allows the libraries to expand the chat service beyond reference to connect students with other departments they might need to get information from, such as the Circulation or Media Department. The transfer feature allows patrons

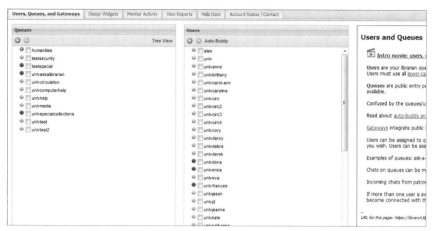

FIGURE 4.2
LibraryH3lp Queue Feature

to be reassigned to experts (either subject or departmental) whenever needed, eliminating the need for patrons to know the layout of the organization in order to get the help that they need. LibraryH3lp also offers administrative features for creating accounts and tracking statistics and transcripts.

Adding Text Reference

Prior to the switch to LibraryH3lp, an increase in patrons using cell phones for texting was observed. This, coupled with the introduction of new technologies offering the potential to text with patrons, led to the adoption of text message reference. The libraries initially used Mosio's product Text a Librarian (www .textalibrarian.com) in order to offer this service. Text messaging is not an automatic feature of LibraryH3lp, but it is possible to integrate it into the system. Incoming messages from Text a Librarian were sent to LibraryH3lp, and then staff would click on a link in order to open up the question in the Mosio product. This setup worked fairly well; however, there were a few inefficiencies. Occasionally librarians would not see the link to Text a Librarian and would answer the question in the chat client, which would not be delivered to the patron. Also, technical difficulties would sometimes result in not relaying the messages to the chat client, so librarians would not notice if a text question had been received. These problems, along with the cost of the Mosio product, led to the decision to try a different way to connect with students via text messaging. In spring 2011, the libraries switched to Twilio

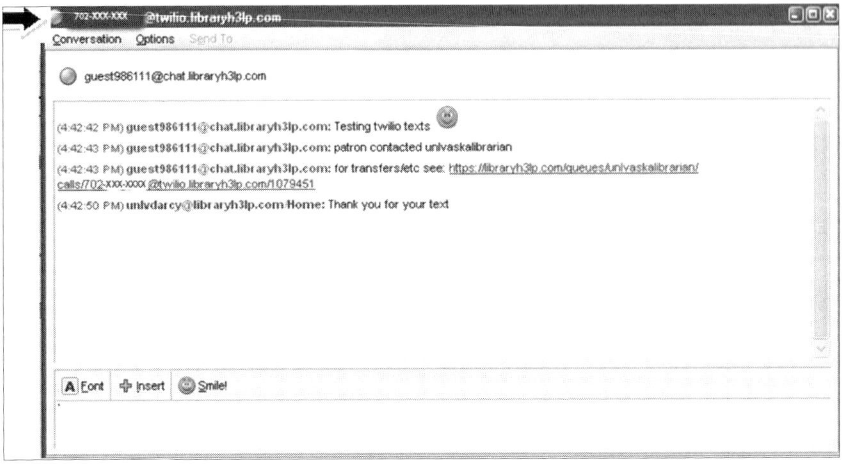

FIGURE 4.3
Twilio Librarian Interface

(www.twilio.com), an option that was far less expensive and better integrated with the LibraryH3lp service. The Twilio subscription provides a local phone number for patrons to text. Messages are received in the LibraryH3lp system and can be answered there. Phone messages inadvertently sent to the text number are rerouted to the Research and Information Desk phone. So far, despite a lack of marketing, this has been working well. An example of the librarian side of Twilio is shown in figure 4.3.

Success with LibraryH3lp

The transition to LibraryH3lp has been hugely successful thus far. Chat statistics have increased 74 percent in the last two years, mostly due to the introduction of the chat widget. The chat widget allows users without instant messaging accounts, or those who do not wish to sign into their accounts, the ability to chat with library staff directly from the chat widget box on the library website. LibraryH3lp has provided us with a nearly seamless communication tool for assisting students and other library users at their immediate point of need. We are ready with the ability to answer quick questions, point them to resources such as research databases, and send relevant links or files to them. The widget is included on every page of the main library website, making it easy for users to find, connect to, and use chat reference.

Incremental Enhancements

As evident in the history above, virtual reference service at the university libraries was incrementally improved over time. The ultimate evolution of the service resulted from being responsive to patron and staff needs. By paying attention to several factors, we were able to position ourselves to best meet patron needs. The following items made the transition possible and could be useful to any library that is ready to update virtual reference services.

EVALUATE, ASSESS, AND UPGRADE

After implementing a new chat reference service, it is important to continually reassess the program. Assessment can be formal or informal and should come from both library staff and from patrons. Surveys, focus groups, and statistics all provide information that can be useful for determining future directions for chat reference services. It is also possible to make use of campus resources. For instance, at UNLV, the Office of Information Technology surveys students about their technology use. From this survey it was able to be determined that students were frequently using smart phones to access campus information, making that an important place for the library to try and integrate its resources. Knowing the technologies that patrons are using and how the chat service is meeting their needs can help to identify future directions for the chat service.

In addition to assessing user needs, library staff input is also very important for the success of the chat reference service and can help to shape the direction of the service. If technical difficulties impede staff from answering questions, then the service cannot be successful. Staff input was one reason for our move away from QuestionPoint. Library staff reported that the product was not stable and questions would be dropped, frustrating both librarian and patron. Also, certain features of the system—such as co-browsing—proved to be too cumbersome to implement. Moving to instant messaging helped solve these problems, making staff more successful in answering patron queries. With the implementation of instant messaging new issues came up, including finding ways to monitor multiple chat clients at one time, trying to staff the service with more than one librarian, and keeping transcripts and statistics. Again staff frustration and technical difficulties were holding back the program, spurring librarians to research alternate possibilities.

Through a process of continuous evaluation by staff and patrons, the libraries were able to improve services as needed. Since assessment is continuous, changes are more gradual, which can be less stressful to both staff and patrons.

Discovering the New

Just as ongoing assessment is needed, it is also essential for someone on staff to remain aware of the changing landscape of technologies available. Keeping apprised of what products are available in the marketplace helps to quickly implement new features when user or staff needs emerge. Occasionally user needs may necessitate a move to an entirely new system, but more often different add-ons can easily be adapted to the current system to quickly and incrementally enhance the service.

When implementing the chat reference service, an important consideration is to know what technologies patrons are currently using. Since the adoption of new technologies shifts over time, it is important to stay aware of what our patrons are currently using. Initially, having a proprietary chat service was suitable for our clientele, but eventually it became clear that patrons were actively using instant messaging and preferred to receive help in that environment rather than logging into a new system. As time went on there was a shift away from instant messaging, with more of our students using cell phones to text. Knowing the technology trends helped place the service where it would get used by patrons with the fewest barriers to entry.

Training

As with any new service, training is important both as the service starts up and as new features are added. Even after the service has been in place for a while, it is important to hold refresher training to reacquaint current staff with all the available features of the system and to get new staff up to speed. Virtual reference training requires both technology training and training to help staff transfer their reference skills into the online synchronous environment.

At the university libraries different types of training were undertaken. Big-picture overviews of the new service were provided, with explanations of how the service fits into the current reference offerings and what the philosophy toward the service would be. How-to and one-on-one training sessions were also held, to ensure that staff could handle the technical aspects of the service and that they effectively answer reference questions via chat. Training not only updates people and makes them proficient at using the system, but also builds confidence and makes people more comfortable in staffing the service.

THE FUTURE OF VIRTUAL REFERENCE AT UNLV

Chat reference services have been increasingly popular at the university libraries. The service has changed greatly since it was first discussed in 2002, adapting when needed to new patron and staff demands. The service will continue to change as new needs arise and new technologies become available. The future of the libraries' virtual reference includes reshaping it to expand our current chat service beyond Research and Information (R & I) staff to include other library service points, such as Circulation and Special Collections, so that specialized chat questions that are best answered outside R & I can be transferred accordingly. Staff training is currently under way to expand and improve the service.

In order to provide the best user services that the UNLV Libraries and their staff can offer, it is both progressive and useful to learn to connect with our University's students in ways that synchronize with their favored modes of communication. In recent years, this has meant making ourselves readily available to them through chat, texting, and social networking applications. Many technology-based services are being investigated or considered at UNLV Libraries, but our chat reference service continues to grow steadily in popularity and use and it is anticipated that virtual reference will be around in some form for many years to come.

> **Making the Successful Transition to LibraryH3lp: Key Factors**
> - Trial and error
> - Incremental enhancements
> - Evaluation and feedback
> - Staff training
> - Awareness of current trends
> - Changes based on user and staff needs
> - Chat widgets on all web pages

REFERENCE

UNLV Libraries. 2008. Instant Messaging Statistics Generator: History of the IM statistics generator. Web and Digitization Services. www.library.unlv.edu/wds/download/#history

Instant Messaging for Virtual Reference

Beth Thomsett-Scott

U se of instant messaging tools is constantly increasing among all segments of the population. Many of these tools are free and can be an integral and vital part of a library's virtual reference suite of resources. This chapter will provide details on establishing a chat reference service drawing upon the UNT Libraries experience with Meebo. With the purchase of Meebo by Google in June 2012, many libraries, including the UNT Libraries, are seeking alternatives. Based on suggestions from several electronic discussions lists, a brief discussion of alternatives to this popular service will also be provided.

Selecting an IM service requires a variety of decisions points. Often the first decision is whether to go with a free or fee-based product. Free software is desirable due to budget constraints. However, as with other products, fee-based services frequently provide additional features and more stability. Another important feature of instant messaging software is whether items are web-based or require a download, especially from the patron side. Web-based products ensure that there is no possibility of viruses through downloads (Gordon and Stephens 2007). Additionally, there are fewer firewall or security issues because these products usually use their own servers to store account transcripts and other information. The web-based nature of these products also allows staff to log in from any computer, as well as from home or other locations as needed.

Some instant messaging softwares include a multiprotocol option that permits the aggregation of other IM accounts, such as Google Talk and AIM, into a single account page. Without an aggregator, libraries would have to have accounts for each of the popular IM platforms, and users would have to establish accounts or create accounts in these services to chat with the library staff. Some libraries maintain multiple IM accounts to allow users to "buddy" them and use the aggregator software to facilitate responses; thus, only one browser window is required. Without an aggregator, a separate browser window or tab is required for each

FIGURE 5.1
Subject Guide Widget—American University Library

service or the library is limited to one service and has to guess which might prove to be the most popular service. With the proliferation of IM services, selecting only one can be extremely limiting. Staff can use the aggregator as a one-stop shopping place to receive and answer questions. In addition to aggregating accounts from other services, oftentimes multiple accounts can be created in the aggregator for different purposes, such as accounts for individual subject librarians or library departments. Some nonaggregating IM services provide this option as well.

One of the standard features that are highly desired for libraries is the option for users to send off-line messages. While service may not be provided 24/7, this does allow users to leave messages and contact information and receive responses when staff logs in the next morning.

To further assist users, many libraries moved to embedded chat, where a widget or chat box plug-in from their IM system of choice was put on their pages to instantly allow users to connect to library staff (Northrup 2008). Widgets are frequently customizable and serve to allow users to immediately type in a question and be connected to a library staff member; thus, providing the user with seamless access to library help. Many libraries include widgets on their subject guides, class pages, and other reference pages (fig. 5.1). Widgets can also be added to Facebook pages and other sites where users might find them. A good example of a Facebook widget is provided by the Seattle Public Library (fig. 5.2). Some libraries include the widget on all library pages for enhanced patron access. Additional suggestions for strategically locating widgets are provided by Northrup (2008).

69

FIGURE 5.2
Facebook Widget—Seattle Public Library

Some IM software will allow multiple widgets to be created for particular purposes, such as help pages, subject guides, or catalog pages; or for particular people, including subject librarians, circulation department, branch libraries, and other areas. Be sure to check how many widgets can be created and how many patrons can use a widget simultaneously.

Widget creation usually follows similar steps. Enter the name for the widget that should be something logical to patrons since this is what they see on the pages and the display name. Best practice is that all widgets have a similar naming standard. Most software will show you what the widget will look like as you create it to avoid any mistakes. Of course, widgets can be edited and new ones created as needed. Select from predetermined color schemes or customize to your organization. As with any service, virtual or physical, it is best to brand the widget with organizational colors and images. Depending on the software used, additional customization options may be available. Usually, the widget development process will end with the generation of a piece of HTML code. The widget HTML code can

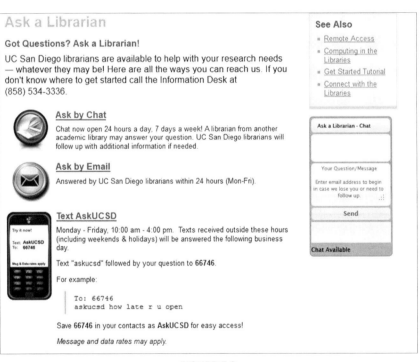

FIGURE 5.3
Leave E-mail Message—University of California at San Diego Library

then be pasted onto a web page resulting in an embedded widget. Often Flash is used to make this happen. The widget can be set to show the library staff as online or off-line, with the option to add a message such as "Leave an off-line message if librarian is not available." Figure 5.3 shows an image of the IM chat widget with instructions for patrons to provide an e-mail in case of disconnection which is useful idea. Patrons are also anonymous, which helps with sensitive topics (Wagner 2007) and thus is an advantage over systems requiring users to identify themselves. Users can create a nickname or use the guest name provided by the widget.

Transactions may be lost when patrons go to another page, usually by clicking on URLs sent by the librarians. As well as encouraging patrons to copy and paste the URL, libraries can provide options to open a widget window rather than using the embedded widget. Options include providing a pop-out widget or the opening of a separate page for the widget, as shown in figure 5.4. The latter somewhat reduces the value of the widget because users have to click on a link and then are able to IM the library staff.

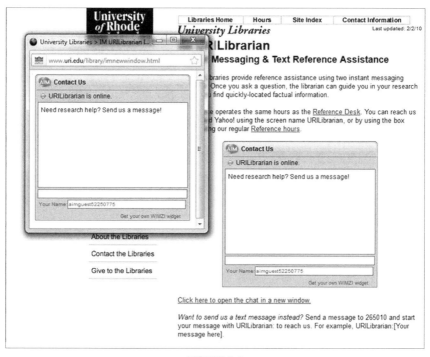

FIGURE 5.4
Pop-Out Widget—University of Rhode Island Libraries

Users may be confused by the widget, however, since it seems to indicate to some that staff are available just by the presence of the widget. Wagner (2007) and Breitbach, Mallard, and Sage (2009) note that libraries can write a script to hide the widget when staff are not available. As an alternative, the message users see can be adjusted to encourage them to leave their question and contact information when a staff member is not online.

Additional items to keep in mind when selecting a tool are the number of concurrent operators (i.e., library staff) able to log in at one time, limits to the number of widgets able to be created, limits to the number of patrons able to use a particular widget, automatic recording of transcripts, ability to send URLs, and the presence of a spellcheck option.

OVERVIEW OF INSTANT MESSAGING REFERENCE AT THE UNIVERSITY OF NORTH TEXAS

In summer 2009, the Research and Instructional Services (RIS) department of the University of North Texas Libraries implemented a beta test of Meebo Messenger as a potential addition to their suite of virtual reference tools. After testing through the summer and allowing a few key personnel to get familiar with the system, the libraries took the offering live in the fall semester. Coverage was provided from 10 a.m. to 8 p.m. Monday through Thursday, 10 a.m. to 5 p.m. on Friday, and from 1 to 5 p.m. on Saturdays and Sundays. A revised Ask Us page was developed to accommodate the widget and to provide links to the other virtual services, as well as a Serve Yourself section linking to subject guides, tutorials, and other helpful tools. In fall 2011, a separate account for the Discovery Park Campus was created.

Implementing and Maintaining an Instant Messaging Service

Training

Staff members were provided with basic training and given the chance to practice with other staff. Since most staff members were already familiar with the Messenger service (Messenger was initially implemented to serve as a communication mechanism for staff before being replaced by Microsoft Communicator), training was very straightforward. Emphasis was on effective communication using IM. A "quick tips" card was developed that contained log-in information and reminders. A greeting is considered imperative, such as "Hello, I'm Beth. How may I help you?" As with all services, the goal of the IM service is to instruct the patrons rather than simply providing information. Once it was known that users accidently left the IM page by clicking on URLs provided by staff, users were instructed to open another browser window and copy and paste the URL. Additionally, staff members were requested to guide users to pages and not just provide URLs. Staff is given thorough training on customer service, UNT Libraries policies, catalog use, and electronic resources, as well as suggestions for when to use Wikipedia, Google, Google Scholar, and similar, as done for face-to-face and other virtual services training.

Staffing

As mentioned earlier, the Reference Unit staff work the virtual and physical reference desks. Staff had the choice of participating in virtual service so long as the best service was being provided by those who were comfortable with the virtual medium. Not all libraries have this luxury. However, due to its simplicity, Meebo was fairly easy for even the most "virtually fearful" staff member to work with, and most IM systems, even the vendor-based systems such as LibraryH3lp, are intuitive and relatively straightforward.

In general, shifts are only two hours long. Staff can ask someone to fill in for them if a quick break is needed. Weekend shifts are four hours long. Both staff and students are required to work on projects and other professional activities during the shifts.

RIS staff members do not work on the reference desk while monitoring our multiple (up to four) virtual services. The Discovery Park Library is more specialized, serving the needs of the College of Information and the College of Engineering, and has significantly lower traffic; thus, reference desk staff currently monitors the IM account. From the author's discussions with librarians at other libraries—particularly smaller college and public libraries—desk staff often monitor IM and treat virtual users as they do regular patrons. For example, if an operator is with another patron, they ask the IM patron to send the question and let them know they are working with another patron and that there will be a short wait time. If a walk-up or phone patron arrives in the middle of an IM question, they are asked to wait until the IM patron is satisfied. In sum, regardless of the medium, patrons are handled in the order they arrive. However, just as with face-to-face patrons, it may be possible to work with several patrons at once or to triage basic questions.

Evaluating and Assessing

The UNT Libraries use an online reference statistics program where questions and answers are recorded. This easily permits supervisors to evaluate the quality of the responses by staff in order to determine if additional training is needed in IM techniques, subject knowledge, library policies, or other issues. Additionally, supervisors can review trends in questions to better prepare staff for questions about class assignments and frequently occurring questions. Reports are prepared regularly to show usage based on a variety of queries, such as day, week, time, librarian, and duration. Instant messaging transaction numbers generally grew with time, although it still has fairly low traffic compared to walk-up patrons.

Staff members work on other activities while monitoring IM and the other virtual services. In general, most staff use their virtual reference time as an opportunity to catch up on current awareness, filing, e-mail cleanup, and similar activities that could be easily stopped when a patron entered one of the virtual services and effectively resumed after assisting the patron.

Questions received through the IM service crossed all boundaries although the majority were traditional reference:"I need articles," "I need books," "How do I use x database." This is similar to the results of Breitbach, Mallard, and Sage (2009), who reported that 80 percent of questions received required professional assistance—how to use the databases, search the catalog, and the like—rather than being of a simple directional nature. Only 3.7 percent of their transactions were directional (e.g., "How do I get to the library?" "Can you give me the number for advising?").

The UNT Libraries did not perform a staff survey. Anecdotal evidence indicated that most staff felt that the IM option was a good addition to the virtual reference suite of tools. There were some concerns with missed chats and patrons needing faster responses than face-to-face patrons. The latter is likely due to a comfort level with the IM medium. RIS and DP staff members are encouraged to ask for patron e-mails if the question begins to drag on or if follow-up is needed. For questions where patrons will likely need additional help later or where patrons did not want to stay for further instructions, staff is asked to provide the e-mail addresses for the reference areas. An example of this is an upper-level science student who wants to know which database to use to find engineering information but does not want to wait for the "how to use it well" tutorial. Staff give a few quick tips and then end with a "please contact us if we can help further" and the Discovery Park reference e-mail. There are numerous instances of compliments from students about the convenience and value of the service, and a high rate of thank-you messages. Breitbach, Mallard, and Sage (2009) report similar findings through a staff survey. One interesting comment is that some staff felt that students would provide more honest feedback through IM than face-to-face (e.g., through the use of emoticons, or requests for further help or more details).

The availability of the widgets on various pages prevent staff from determining where users come from—in library, on campus, or remotely. As well, because users do not need to provide any information, staff cannot ascertain whether the patron is affiliated with UNT. However, neither of these statistics is considered problematic enough not to use the widgets.

Marketing

As with many libraries, marketing is a challenge. Widgets are included on all subject guides. Initially subject librarians had the widgets set to their own accounts and monitored the widget when available. However, it was decided that librarians could also link to the Ask Us chat widget and have all questions go through the staff member monitoring the service. The widgets are included as part of the content for the guides thus minimizing effort on behalf of the subject librarians. The Discovery Park Library (DPL) had the widget embedded on the content sidebar, which shows on all DPL pages. The UNT Libraries Ask Us page serves as a landing area for patrons where they then select the virtual or physical service of interest. A link to Ask Us is provided on all library pages. When the reference desks staffed by RIS members are closed, there are large signs advertising the availability of virtual reference services. With many ways to reach users (and nonusers), libraries need to select a variety of advertising methods that reach diverse groups of people. Advertising on the libraries' website and in-library reaches current users while advertising through flyers, newspapers, exterior banners reach both current and nonusers. Additional promotional methods are provided by Breitbach, Mallard, and Sage (2009) and the Suggested Reading section contains some useful starting points for libraries looking to begin or enhance their marketing.

Visit www.libsuccess.org/index.php?title=Online_Reference#Software_We _Like_for_IM_Reference for other IM users and information on their services.

INSTANT MESSAGING SUCCESS
IN VIRTUAL REFERENCE SERVICES

The UNT Libraries found Meebo, especially with the Meebo Me widget, to be an effective free tool with which to offer effective virtual reference. There was minimal setup and staff training time. The interface was easy for both staff and patrons to use. With the loss of Meebo, libraries are beginning to replace their IM software. The next section collects IM software suggestions for including in-library virtual reference services. The suggestions come from several electronic discussion lists, including Web4Lib and LIBREF-L.

POSSIBLE REPLACEMENTS FOR MEEBO

The sale of Meebo and resulting unavailability of Messenger and the Meebo Widget are serious concerns to libraries. There are a number of possible options available. Due to printing deadlines, I was unable to test many of the products. Where possible, I've added in content from their sites and personal observations from other librarians using the software to help with decision making.

Adium

For Macs. Server-based free aggregator. Visit http://adium.im for more information.

Chatango

Flash based, so not available for mobile tools. Visit http://chatango.com/ for more information.

Chatwing

Website address needed, limits functionality. No user log-in. Widgets work well. Visit http://chatwing.com for more information.

CraftySyntax

Crafty Syntax is free if you host it on your server or low cost based on the number of visitors to your chat site. Even with the hosted version, the cost is very low. The website (www.craftysyntax.com/index.php) reports that the software is fully customizable, provides widgets, and offers in-depth reporting features.

Digsby

Multiprotocol option. Also offers e-mail notifications and social network options. Visit www.digsby.com for more information.

eBuddy

Free aggregator. Web-based and easy use on mobile devices. Visit www.ebuddy .com for more information.

Google Talk

Download required. Options for mobile devices. Allows voice chat. Visit www .google.com/talk/about.html for more information.

imo

Free aggregator. Widgets availability is not obvious. Web-based and mobile options. Visit https://imo.im/ for more information.

Instant Service

Used by Florida's Tampa Bay Library Consortium and Colorado's AskColorado/ AskAcademic statewide service, InstantService may be an option. At a fairly low cost, InstantService provides IM, widgets, SMS, and a good level of customization. Chapter 8, "AskColorado," discusses the use of InstantService in AskColorado/ AskAcademic. InstantService's main page is located at www.instantservice.com/ solutions/appexchange.html.

LibChat

LibChat (http://support.springshare.com/2012/06/12/meebo-going-away-libchat -coming-your-way-see-it-at-ala/) is a software provided by Springshare, the company that created LibGuides. Libraries that use LibGuides will find that LibChat easily links into LibGuides as a replacement for the Meebo widget. Pricing is based on the number of concurrent operators. LibAnswers is discussed in chapter 1, and LibChat can be incorporated into this product as an additional module.

LibraryH3lp

Chapter 4, "Virtual Reference at UNLV Libraries," discusses the use of LibraryH3lp, and there is a brief overview in chapter 1, "Virtual Reference Service." LibraryH3lp is not free but, since it was developed for libraries, is priced in an affordable manner based on possible client use. Over the years since its inception, I have not heard any negative comments. The providers are responsive to suggestions; the system is flexible and works for academic, public and special libraries; and there is a strong community of users. Additionally, comments on the listserv indicate that the widgets use JavaScript rather than flash, which allows for easy use on mobile phones. Featured advantages include customizable widgets, multiple queues, and unlimited operators.

Pidgin

Pidgin is a free, downloadable aggregator. Prior to Meebo's domination of the free IM aggregator market, Pidgin was a strong candidate. Not web-based. Visit www.pidgin.im/about/ for more information.

Plugo

Visit http://www.plugoo.com/ for more information.

QuestionPoint

QuestionPoint is provided by OCLC and is fairly popular among libraries. Highlights include 24/7 coverage for your patrons through the 24/7 Reference Cooperative, the Qwidget option, and web access. Further details are available at www.oclc.org/questionpoint/about/default.htm.

Olark (Hab.la)

Olark was formerly known as Hab.la. Free for limited use, but best results require a paid version. Visit www.olark.com/?rid=hab.la for more information.

Spark

Hosted and web-based options. Visit www.igniterealtime.org/projects/sparkweb/index.jsp for more information.

Trillian

Free aggregator. Features include mobile compatibility, interoperability with social media sites, and longevity (ten years of development). Visit www.trillian.im for more information.

Zoho

Free aggregator with several different types of embeddable widgets. No apparent notification system, although some people mentioned using Zoho in conjunction with Adium (Macs) or Trillian (PCs). Visit https://chat.zoho.com for more information.

Zopim

Has a free option, but with high traffic the pay version may be required for improved access. The free option provides one operator and a maximum of two concurrent chats. Easy to create and launch widgets. Plug-ins and add-ons for some popular products including Drupal and WordPress. Visit www.zopim.com for more information.

LISTS AND SUMMARIES OF IM SOFTWARES

http://sixrevisions.com/tools/10-free-website-chat-widgets-to-make-your-site-interactive/

http://lisnews.org/meebo_messenger_meebo_me_discontinued_july_11_2012

http://libraryh3lp.blogspot.com/2012/06/meebo-migrations-alternatives-for.html

http://en.wikipedia.org/wiki/Comparison_of_instant_messaging_clients

REFERENCES

Breitbach, William, Matthew Mallard, and Robert Sage. 2009. "Using Meebo's Embedded IM for Academic Reference Services: A Case Study." *References Services Review* 37, no. 1: 83–98.

Gordon, Rachel Singer, and Michael Stephens. 2007. "Embedding a Librarian in Your Web Site Using Meebo." *Computers in Libraries* 27, no. 8: 44–45.

Northrup, Lori. 2008. "Meebo Me! For Embedded Chat Reference: Patron Initiated Encounters without Downloads or Accounts." *College and Undergraduate Libraries* 15, no. 3: 357–363.

Wagner, Cassie. 2007. "Meebo." *The Charleston Advisor* 9, no. 1: 47–48.

Embedded Librarians Using Web 2.0 Services for Reference

Ellen Hampton Filgo

The term *embedded librarianship* came about in 2004, when Barbara Dewey related the concept of wartime embedded journalists to the integration of librarians into physical and virtual educational and research spaces through collaboration with various academic campus partners (Dewey 2004, 6). However, the concept of embedded librarianship has been around for longer than that. It developed from the model of an academic branch library (Drewes and Hoffman 2010) where smaller, focused collections were developed in close collaboration between faculty and librarian. Embedded librarianship expands on that resource development collaboration and adds in research help, information literacy instruction, and reference services.

Embedded librarianship can mean a physical relocation: many librarians have moved out of the library building in order to relocate their offices into the departments or schools that they serve (Kesselman and Watstein 2009). Some haven't relocated an entire office but are still located physically within their user communities through office hours held outside of the library building (Clyde and Lee 2011). However, the majority of the literature on embedded librarianship describes a more virtual embedding.

As colleges and universities have increasingly embraced learning management systems (LMS) for course management as well as created online courses and programs, librarians have sought to embed themselves into these virtual spaces to provide research services and information literacy instruction. Librarians embedded into LMS have done so in many ways. Some provide screencast tutorials, LibGuides, or other online modules to replace a face-to-face instruction session (Held 2010, Tumbleson and Burke 2010); some participate in discussion forums (Matthew and Schroeder 2006) or even create or review student assignments (Bowler and Street 2008, Love and Norwood 2007). Holding live instruction sessions via web conferencing software is another way that librarians have sought to virtually embed themselves into the classroom (Love and Norwood 2007).

As the librarians describe these varied experiments with embedded librarianship, one refrain comes through loud and clear. It is vitally important to closely collaborate with the instructors of the courses in which the embedding takes place (Clyde and Lee 2011, Owens 2008, Drewes and Hoffman 2010). Some suggest that the very definition of *embedded* must include such "purposeful collaborations" (Bowler and Street 2008, 439).

As the use of the LMS increases in higher education, and librarians keep experimenting and collaborating in order to embed their services within it, another movement in higher education has been growing. This movement criticizes LMS courses as "walled gardens" (Mott 2010) and advocates for the use of Web 2.0 technologies and services as a platform for teaching and learning (EDUCAUSE Learning Initiative 2009)—both in strictly online courses as well as traditional face-to-face classrooms.

Web 2.0 advocates note the open, collaborative nature of social media and new media tools that allow students to be more involved in their own learning process (Stern and Willits 2011). They see social media as putting "the role of educators in a completely different light to correspond with the new paradigm shift from teacher/curriculum-centered education to learner/student-centered education" (Tadros 2011, 86). Education in an open, online digital medium would mean that students would "frame, curate, share and direct" their own learning (Campbell 2009). Web 2.0 connects a learner-focused pedagogy with a user-focused technology; content and construct can merge together; student learning can happen collaboratively and openly on the public Web.

This chapter will feature a Web 2.0 embedded librarian project at Baylor University, detail a few other similar projects, and describe a variety of the Web 2.0 tools commonly used in teaching and learning.

WEB 2.0 EMBEDDED LIBRARIAN PROJECT AT BAYLOR UNIVERSITY LIBRARIES

Introduction

In the spring of 2009, I watched an exciting YouTube video produced by Dr. Monica Rankin of University of Texas–Dallas, who had been using Twitter to facilitate discussion among the students of her history survey course. The video can be found at http://www.youtube.com/watch?v=Cz_W6vmrjmI. Reflecting on the video, I thought that the idea of using Twitter in a classroom was an interesting experiment and thought that perhaps including a reference librarian in the Twitter stream would provide some of those "just-in-time" answers to questions that invariably come up during class discussions. The librarian could point to further resources and readings as well as answer quick factual information.

Class Design

That summer, I brought the video and the idea of an embedded librarian via Twitter to the attention of Dr. Gardner Campbell, then Baylor University's director of the Academy for Teaching and Learning, and professor of Literature and Media in the Honors College. Dr. Campbell responded positively, and I was invited to join the class for two semesters, fall 2009 and fall 2010. The class I was embedded into was a first-year honors seminar called "From Memex to YouTube: Introduction to New Media Studies." The focus of the class was to understand the field of new media studies and learn about "the past and future of computers and how they affect how we think and what we do." Because a central learning goal for this class was for students not just to study new media but to also participate in it, Dr. Campbell required his students to robustly use a number of Web 2.0 applications and technologies. The students were required to blog their reflections on the readings before every class, comment substantively on another classmate's blog, contribute to the class wiki, tag links of interest using Delicious.com, and participate in a class discussion using Twitter (using a designated class hashtag). The class's virtual participation was then aggregated into what Dr. Campbell called "the motherblog" (fig. 6.1). Using the WordPress blogging software and a couple of key plug-ins, this site brought together all the students' blog posts, recent comments, Delicious links, and Tweets. It was the dashboard (user interface) for the class's learning experience.

From Memex to YouTube, Fall 2010

Recognizing the Gift

HOME   ABOUT

SEARCH THE MOTHERBLOG

To search, type and hit enter

DELICIOUS NEW MEDIA, FALL 2010

- The Information Palace by James Gleick | NYRBlog | The New York Review of Books December 9, 2010 [...] *lnboz*
- What the DoD's PlayStation-powered Condor Cluster means for the future of supercomputing - SmartPlanet December 7, 2010 [...] *fastsoccerskier25*
- Family Force 5 - Wikipedia, the free encyclopedia December 5, 2010 [...] *domfromtexas*
- make a definition December 5, 2010 [...] *domfromtexas*
- Last.fm vs Pandora - Difference and Comparison | Diffen December 5, 2010 [...] *domfromtexas*
- Facebook vs MySpace - Rivalries - Newsweek 2010 December 5, 2010 [...] *domfromtexas*
- Spanish Woman Claims She Now Owns Sun December 2, 2010 /facepalm [...] *arpit_desai*

---

just finished my essay

December 11th, 2010 by colorblind in Uncategorized · No Comments

and I am sad now. I can't believe this class just ended.

Comments Off

Last presentations

December 9th, 2010 by fastskier25 in Uncategorized · baylor_nms_f10 · No Comments

I just realized I hadn't blogged for the final presentations, which i must say were pretty amazing. It definitely was awesome that they both chose to do a music related project without even planning it. I've never tried last.fm but it sounds pretty cool and I think I might start using it. I've used pandora on my itouch before and really liked it, and I think last.fm will probably work even better. Jan's project was really cool too, I've never used myspace before and the music function of it looks really useful. I kind of wish facebook had something similar, but that may never happen. Well this class has been awesome, and I'll miss all of you conceptacular colleagues next semester. Good luck to all on the final, adios.

Comments Off

Final Blog

December 6th, 2010 by raminator08 in Uncategorized · No Comments

Great projects guys. Great way to end a great semester with a great class. I had a great time in this class. I learned so many great things. Everything was great.

Forgot my works cited for the project.

Works Cited

Barnes, Susan B. "Alan Kay: Transforming the Computer into a Communication Medium."   *IEEE Annals of the History of Computing*. IEEE Computer Society, 2007. Print.

Engelbart, Douglas. "Augmenting Human Intellect." Kay, Alan and Adele Goldberg. "Personal   Dynamic Media." ." *The New Media Reader*. Ed. Noah Wardrip-Fruin and Nick   Montfort. London: MIT Press, 2003. Print.

COURSE SYLLABUS (BETA)

The course syllabus is here.

SITEWIDE COMMENTS

COMMENTS FOR DOCTOR ICTHARYYN' SING-ALONG BLOG » COMMENT ON GLITCHES BY LORIANN SCHWART
Posted 30 hours ago

The Nintendo Wii started out the revolution of movement primarily based gaming management, but they had been not the 1st. The Sony PS3 remotes have had gyroscopes in the remote ... [Link]

COMMENTS FOR FREEDOM FIGHTER FIGHTS FOREST FIRES » COMMENT ON AIRBEAR-THE BANE OF MY EXISTENCE BY JOCURI ONLINE
Posted 5 days ago

I was just browsing for relevant entries for my project research and I happened to find yours, very informative blog post [Link]

COMMENTS FOR BEARS IN THE INTERWEBZ » COMMENT ON ALWAYS ATTEMPTING ACCURATE AND AUTOMATIC ANNOTATION BY 3STH3R
Posted 4 weeks ago

With some of the no blast results, I think it is safe to conclude that our Benedict will have some cool new proteins~ [Link]

FIGURE 6.1

The Motherblog

Embedding the Librarian

As the embedded librarian, the primary way I interacted with the class was through Twitter comments during the class period. At the beginning of the class, the students were instructed to take out their laptops, log in to Twitter, and greet the librarian. This not only got them used to using Twitter to interact with me, but was also a signal from Dr. Campbell that their use of laptop computers was for learning. As the class progressed, the students would tweet their comments, questions, nuggets of information that they gleaned from the readings and any other tidbits. As they tweeted, they would use the class's designated hashtag (fall 2009: #nmsf09, fall 2010: #nms_f10). Across campus, in my office, I would open up TweetDeck (a popular Twitter application) and follow along, using a search for the hashtag to pull together all the students' tweets, as indicated in figure 6.2. I would often interact with the students via Twitter, using the hashtag and @-replies to pull my tweets into the conversation.

My contributions via Twitter during the class were broad and varied, as shown in figure 6.3. I linked to everything from books in our catalog and articles in our library's subscription databases to Wikipedia articles and YouTube videos. Often I explored the author of the reading they were assigned, looking up background information, biographies, other articles or books they had written or other sources that cited or referenced the author. Even if a student tweeted something that seemed to veer off the topic of class conversation, I often tried to link to something along those lines as well, as I wanted to encourage any connections the student might be making between the reading, the class discussion, and their own personal knowledge.

I also was embedded into the class via the students' blogs. At the beginning of the semester, I subscribed to the motherblog's main RSS feed in order to keep up with the students' writing. I commented often on their posts, excited to be seeing the beginning inklings of what their final projects would end up to be. Sometimes I was able to provide resources to help them with their projects through commenting on their posts.

The class was required to bookmark links of interest using Delicious.com (http://delicious.com), all marked with a designated class tag as well as any other subject or topic tags of their choice. I would also bookmark interesting links; sometimes some of the links I would send through Twitter during the class period. All these links were pulled into the motherblog through the RSS feed generated by the class tag.

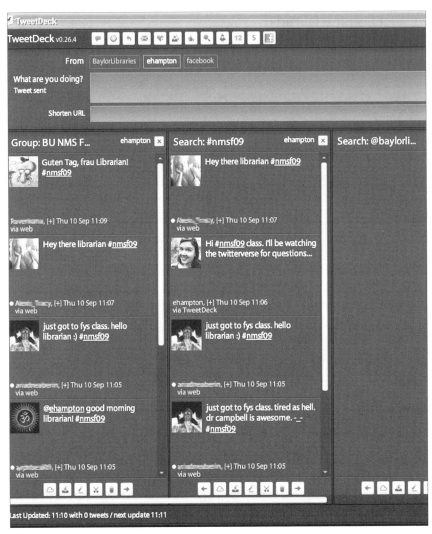

FIGURE 6.2

TweetDeck Conversation

FIGURE 6.3
Twitter Conversation

There were several times during the semester that the class met in Second Life. Our variously costumed virtual characters met together, discussed the readings, occasionally had to interact with curious other Second Life residents, and explored some of the interesting educational spaces that Second Life has to offer.

Response

After each semester was over, I conducted an informal survey using the form feature in Google Docs to gauge how the students felt about having a librarian embedded into their class. The survey reported that the students' attitude toward interacting with a librarian via Twitter, their blogs, and the rest of the tools they used was overwhelmingly positive. They reported that they often clicked on the Twitter links that I sent to help them better understand the topic of discussion. One student stated, "The librarian's participation was a critical part of the class because [she] was able to provide outside resources and spend time looking for those resources that proved relevant to the class, a task which students would be unlikely to do at all, much less during a class." All the students indicated that they felt more knowledgeable about library resources after this class experience, including resources such as "chat, online resources and the librarians themselves." The interaction with the students even went beyond the Web 2.0 tools used specifically for class. On their own initiative, they created a Facebook group (to which I was invited) where they often planned study groups.

I met with students outside of web space as well. The students booked appointments with me for further help with projects for the class and for other classes, and sought me out on Twitter, on Facebook, and over e-mail with questions. The students called me "our librarian" (one class even called me "guardian librarian"), as I truly became *the* go-to person for any kind of research help. Through this experience, I felt that I was embedded more naturally and richly in the class and their academic lives online.

OTHER EXAMPLES OF WEB 2.0 EMBEDDED LIBRARIANS

Librarians have unabashedly embraced Web 2.0 for many purposes: marketing and communications, creating community and conversation among library patrons, and making library resources more easily findable and shareable. Beyond those reasons, librarians are finding Web 2.0 tools and applications to be ideal for information literacy instruction. In fact, a recent study found that 84 percent of librarians who use Web 2.0 tools do so as a part of their instruction with students (Luo 2010, 37). A few examples of this type of instruction follow.

Michael Stephens, assistant professor in the School of Library and Information Science at San Jose State University, used the WordPress blogging software—specifically, the social network–oriented BuddyPress package of plug-ins—to create an alternative to an LMS (Jones 2011). He successfully used WordPress for several graduate level library school courses at Dominican University. The class also used Twitter with a designated class hashtag to connect the students. The BuddyPress software is shown in action in figure 6.4.

A group of librarians at Miami University in Oxford, Ohio, teaching a course called "Information Studies in the Digital Age" used Ning.com to re-create a traditional LMS using the features that Ning provides: "the blogs, discussion boards, and group pages; the posting of podcasts, images, and videos; and the integration of RSS feeds, widgets and Twitter" (Sullivan et al. 2010, 3). Joan Petit and Amanda Click, instruction librarians at the American University in Cairo, revamped a

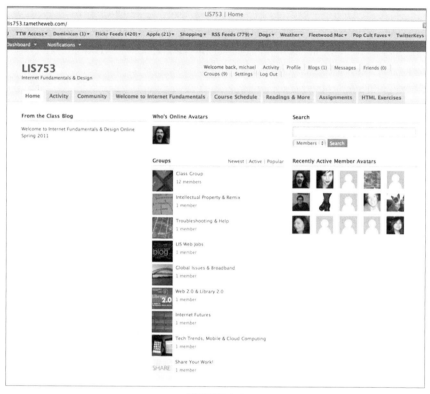

FIGURE 6.4
BuddyPress Example

standard library instruction credit course into a class which utilized wikis and blogs to inspire interactivity and student learning (Petit and Click 2010).

The library literature is full of case studies of librarians experimenting with Web 2.0 technologies for the purpose of library instruction and information literacy; however, using Web 2.0 to embed a librarian into a classroom in collaboration with a nonlibrary instructor is not that common. A few exceptional examples stand out and are described below.

Over the course of a few semesters, Marian Davis and Carol Smith, librarians at the University of Central Missouri, embedded themselves into several different courses (Digital Africana, English Composition, and African-American Literature) that were being offered solely via Second Life, the 3-D virtual world (Davis and Smith 2009). Throughout the semester, they provided a series of instruction sessions focused on the research process that closely followed the course curriculum. Despite technological problems and a challenging learning curve, the librarians persisted with their embedded project and planned to continue it in order to further study whether it was an effective tool for instruction.

Buffy J. Hamilton, school media specialist at Creekview High School in Canton, Georgia, has been running a significant project in Web 2.0 embedded librarianship since 2009, called Media 21 (Hamilton 2011a). In this program, Hamilton has collaborated very closely with English teacher Susan Lester and has used numerous Web 2.0 tools in order to engage students in participatory learning. The students built research portals using NetVibes (www.netvibes.com), a Web 2.0 publishing platform that uses a dashboard approach, allowing for easy embedding of RSS feeds, videos, blogs, calendars, Google searches, and other widgets of content from around the Web. An example of the NetVibes class is shown in figure 6.5. The students also used blogs to document their research and information evaluation processes. In order to collaborate on writing projects, the students used Google Docs and a wiki to review their fellow students' portfolios. Hamilton and Lester also encouraged the use of some Web 2.0 multimedia tools such as Glogster (www .glogster.com), Xtranormal (www.xtranormal.com), VoiceThread (www.voicethread .com), and Masher (www.masher.com) and bookmarking and capture tools like EverNote (www.evernote.com) and Diigo (www.diigo.com) (Hamilton 2011b). Hamilton found that her role embedded within the classroom using Web 2.0 was as a partner in a sometimes messy but ultimately rewarding participatory learning process (Hamilton 2011a).

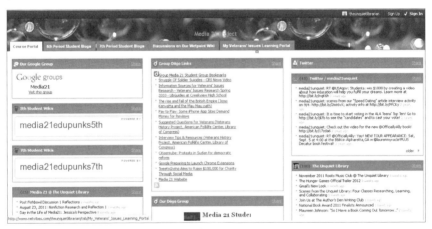

FIGURE 6.5
NetVibes "Classroom"

Librarians continue to explore embedded librarianship, particularly in virtual ways within traditional LMS platforms. Librarians have also increasingly embraced Web 2.0 tools to promote information literacy instruction. The combination of being embedded into classrooms through Web 2.0 tools is an avenue ripe for further investigation. In order to embed, it is vitally important to seek out and collaborate with professors, instructors, and teachers who are committed to student-centered pedagogies and participatory learning and who are either already using these tools in their classrooms or are open to the possibilities.

If you are thinking of initiating or enhancing a current program of embedded librarianship using Web 2.0 tools, please keep the following points in mind.

> **Collaboration.** Find professors, instructors or teachers with whom you can partner. These teachers may or may not already be using Web 2.0 tools in their instruction. Whether they are or not, find collaborators who are committed to flexibility as you try out new ideas, experiment with new tools, and explore new ways for you to teach and for your students to learn.

> **Pedagogy.** Web 2.0 is by its nature open and participatory. Keep in mind that embedded classrooms lend themselves to an open and participatory pedagogy. Delivering a lecture in a classroom is a way of teaching that can be translated into Web 2.0—for example, delivering a lecture via a YouTube video. However, YouTube will also make that lecture available for embedding, sharing, and remixing. Using Web 2.0 tools will change your pedagogy, and you must keep this in mind.

> **Library.** This collaboration is between the library and a traditional instructor in a discipline. Make sure to define what the librarian's role is in the partnership. Are you there to teach how to use the Web 2.0 tools? To teach information literacy concepts? Could it be both? Could it be something completely different?

> **Purpose.** What Web 2.0 tools will you use? Look through your instructional goals to see what types of these tools match up with what skills or concepts you want the students to learn.

With those key points in mind, this next section will guide you through a number of Web 2.0 tools, what their purposes are, and how they have been used in libraries.

WEB 2.0 TOOLS

Blogs

Blogs are one of the oldest Web 2.0 applications, having begun in the late 1990s and popularized with the creation of the Blogger product in 1999. Blogger was subsequently purchased by Google in 2003. Blogs are websites that are updated regularly—usually with easy-to-use blogging software—and contain links, news, commentary, or thoughts. While many blogs function as a type of online diary, blogs can also have a particular focus: politics, music, travel, technology, or business, just to name a very few. Politicians and pundits were early adopters of blogs in order to disseminate their policies or viewpoints and to garner votes for elections. Companies have embraced blogging and often blog as a marketing or public relations tool to promote their products or brand. Libraries have also begun blogging as a way to connect to patrons, promote resources and events, and describe services. While academics themselves have been blogging about their research topics and teaching experiments for a long time, institutional academia has taken a longer time to embrace the practice. However, more recently some schools have provided blogging platforms for their entire student and faculty population. Blogs @ Penn State (http://blogs.psu.edu), a homegrown platform based on the Movable Type blogging software), is a notable example. Companies such as Edublogs (www.edublogs.org) also provide educational blogging to institutions, based upon the open source WordPress blogging software (www.wordpress.com for hosted software, www.wordpress.org for open source, downloadable software).

Twitter

Twitter has recently taken the Web 2.0 world by storm, growing to over 100 million users in September 2011 after launching in 2007 (Twitter 2011). Twitter is a microblogging service that allows its users to quickly post 140-character "tweets" to their followers. Users can post tweets from the Web, via SMS, and through a whole host of third-party applications for desktop or mobile devices. Users find and follow other Twitter users they find interesting and can interact with them through @-replies to and "retweets" (forwards) of their messages. Twitter allows people across the world to find, connect, and share information in real-time. See chapter 2, "Using Twitter for Virtual Reference Services," to find out more about how libraries have embraced Twitter.

Social Bookmarking

Social bookmarking services, such as Delicious.com and Diigo.com, allow users to save, organize, tag, manage, annotate, search, and find links to Internet sites. These services provide a way to save links across more than just one Internet browser, as they are saved on the open Web. What makes this type of bookmarking social is that users can connect with other users they find interesting and follow their bookmarks in order to discover other sites. Diigo.com allows its users to mark up and highlight the web content they bookmark, and to easily share that content within groups. Social bookmarking can be a way to curate web content, and many libraries have begun to use these services to highlight vetted Internet content for their patrons.

Facebook

In the Web 2.0 era, many personal social networking sites, such as Friendster and MySpace, have tried to stake their claim on the landscape; however, it is Facebook that has arisen as the undisputed champion in this area. Facebook presents its users with an easy way to connect with friends, family, and others around them. With a Facebook account, one can share updates, photos, links, and notes. Facebook users can "like" or subscribe to the pages of various businesses, products, celebrities, organizations, and so on, and follow the information that they provide. Users can create groups of like-minded individuals, again for an easy way to share information. Many libraries have created Facebook pages to connect with their patrons, get feedback on materials and services, and promote news and events—Seattle Public Library is an excellent example of a library with a great Facebook page.

Google+ / Google+ Pages

In the summer of 2011, Google launched a new social network called Google+. In developing Google+, the company wanted to fix what they believed was broken about online sharing—the ability to be nuanced about what and with whom people share information. To do so, Google+ introduced *circles*, which guide users into classifying the people they share with, rather than just calling all of them "friends." The idea of circles plus a few other great applications—such as an easy-to-use group video chat, photo sharing, and a slick mobile interface—immediately gave Google+ some diehard fans, and since its launch, it has gained over 40 million users (Evans 2011).

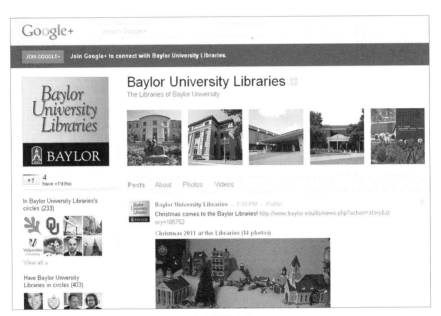

FIGURE 6.6
Google+ Site—Baylor University Libraries

In early November 2011, Google+ launched Google+ Pages, a place where businesses, organizations, and brands could connect with users and customers. This is still fairly new, and libraries have only just begun experimenting with what they can do with Google+. Baylor University Libraries has developed a working Google+ site, as shown in figure 6.6. Some good tips on how to get your library started on Google+ can be found at the blog of David Lee King, Digital Branch and Services manager at the Topeka and Shawnee County (Kansas) Public Library (www.davidleeking.com/2011/11/09/setting-up-a-google-plus-page-for-your-library-is-easy/).

Wikis

A *wiki* is a website that allows for easy editing by a multiple number of users. Wikis usually include a "what you see is what you get" HTML editor and a way to add links to internal wiki pages and external sites very simply. Wikis are often used for collaborative projects, intranets, knowledge bases, and note taking. A main wiki administrator can control access by wiki users to the content, whether it is editing, adding or removing pages, organizing content, and so on. One of the most famous examples of a wiki is Wikipedia (http://www.wikipedia.org), the "free encyclopedia that anyone can edit." There are many types of wiki software; some have to be hosted on a server, such as MediaWiki (Wikipedia runs on this software), and some are hosted on separate websites, like the popular wiki software Wetpaint. Libraries have adopted wikis for uses such as internal knowledge bases and information sharing, quick and collaborative website construction, for archiving policies and procedures, for creating subject guides, community pages and technology help centers (King and Porter 2007, Chu 2009). A good example of a wiki in practice is the Library Success: A Best Practices Wiki (www.libsuccess.org), which provides librarians and others with tips and tricks for using wikis.

Google Docs

Google Docs is an online office suite of software, including word processing, spreadsheets, and presentations. It can be accessed with any Google account username and password. Through Google Docs, users can share documents, collaboratively write and edit them, and store them in the cloud. Users can also review the revision history and download documents in a number of proprietary formats. Another great feature of Google Docs is the ability to create a form or survey that, when submitted to, enters the data into a spreadsheet. Many libraries have taken advantage of this great free software, especially for the survey functionality and collaborative document sharing among library workers.

Ning

Ning.com is a website platform that allows communities to create their own niche social network. It has many of the standard features that users expect of social networks: member profiles, events, groups, forums, and a messaging and chat feature. Ning's strengths are in helping smaller communities find one another through a network tailored for their exact interests. In the library world, smaller interest groups of librarians have taken to Ning, creating sites for librarians interested in teaching and instruction, "Library 2.0," and law librarians, just to name a few. The Library 2.0 Ning site is shown in Figure 6.7.

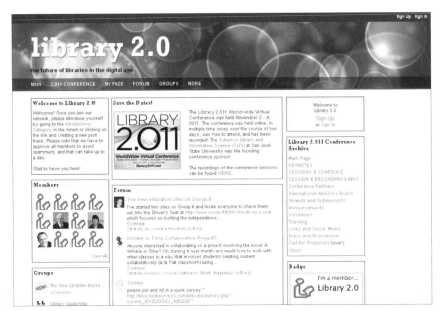

FIGURE 6.7
Library 2.0 Ning Site

Second Life

Second Life is a virtual world that connects its users via 3-D avatar interaction, voice, and text chat. Second Life "residents" (as they are called) explore and interact with one another in this virtual environment. Upon joining Second Life, residents can create their avatar for free, but in order to customize their avatar more fully, or to own or build on any land within Second Life, there is a cost involved. Many educational institutions and libraries have set up a virtual presence within Second Life. The ALA set up their Second Life Presence "ALA Island" in 2007, and has hosted events and book discussions and staffs a reference desk for Second Life residents (ALA Washington Office 2007). The Community Virtual Library is another successful library space within Second Life, hosting exhibits, events, and a busy reference desk staffed by Second Life librarians (Community Virtual Library 2012).

THE FUTURE OF WEB 2.0 TOOLS AND EMBEDDED LIBRARIANSHIP

As you contemplate launching an embedded librarian program in collaboration with other instructional partners, it is important to be flexible as you plan and implement your program, as the current landscape of Web 2.0 tools is diverse and constantly changing. While it can sometimes be a challenge to keep up with the new applications and software coming up over the horizon, it is worth it to bookmark a few websites that can point you to new resources, such as:

- New Media Consortium's Horizon Project (which charts the landscape of emerging technologies for teaching and learning (www.nmc.org/horizon -project/)
- Library 2.0 Ning Community (www.library20.com)
- Web 2.0 School Libraries Ning Community (web20schoollibraries .ning.com)
- Library Success Wiki (www.libsucess.org)

REFERENCES

ALA Washington Office. 2007. "ALA on Second Life." *District Dispatch* (blog). March 7. http://www.districtdispatch.org/2007/03/ala-on-second-life/.

Bowler, Meagan, and Kori Street. 2008. "Investigating the Efficacy of Embedment: Experiments in Information Literacy Integration." *Reference Services Review* 36, no. 4: 438–449.

Campbell, Gardner. 2009. "A Personal Cyberinfrastructure." *EDUCAUSE Review* 44, no. 5: 58–59.

Chu, Samuel Kai-Wah. 2009. "Using Wikis in Academic Libraries." *The Journal of Academic Librarianship* 35, no. 2: 170–176. doi:10.1016/j.acalib.2009.01.004.

Clyde, Jeremie, and Jennifer Lee. 2011. "Embedded Reference to Embedded Librarianship: 6 Years at the University of Calgary." *Journal of Library Administration* 51, no. 4: 389–402. doi:10.1080/01930826.2011.556963.

Community Virtual Library. 2012. *Community Virtual Library*. www.infoisland.org/home/.

Davis, Marian G., and Carol E. Smith. 2009. "Virtually Embedded: Library Instruction within Second Life." *Journal of Library & Information Services in Distance Learning* 3, no. 3/4: 120–137. doi:10.1080/15332900903375465.

Dewey, Barbara I. 2004. "The Embedded Librarian." *Resource Sharing & Information Networks* 17, no. 1/2: 5–17. doi:10.1300/J121v17n01_02.

Drewes, Kathy, and Nadine Hoffman. 2010. "Academic Embedded Librarianship: An Introduction." *Public Services Quarterly* 6, no. 2/3: 75–82. doi:10.1080/15228959.2010.498773.

EDUCAUSE Learning Initiative. 2009. "7 Things You Should Know about Personal Learning Environments." May 12. www.educause.edu/Resources/7ThingsYouShouldKnowAboutPerso/171521.

Evans, Jon. 2011. "I Believe in Google Plus." *TechCrunch* (blog). October 22. http://techcrunch.com/2011/10/22/i-believe-in-google-plus/.

Hamilton, Buffy J. 2011a. "The School Librarian as Teacher: What Kind of Teacher Are You?" *Knowledge Quest* 39, 5: 34–40.

———. 2011b. "Creating Conversations for Learning: School Libraries as Sites of Participatory Culture." *School Library Journal* 27, no. 8: 41–43.

Held, Tim. 2010. "Blending In: Collaborating with an Instructor in an Online Course." *Journal of Library & Information Services in Distance Learning* 4, no. 4: 153–165. doi:10.1080/1533290X.2010.528272.

Jones, Kyle. 2011. "Buddypress, Libraries, and Higher Education: An Interview with Kenley Neufeld and Michael Stevens." *ALA TechSource* (blog), May 9. www.alatechsource.org/blog/2011/05/buddypress-libraries-and-higher-education-an-interview-with-kenley-neufeld-and-michael-

Kesselman, Martin A., and Sarah Barbara Watstein. 2009. "Creating Opportunities: Embedded Librarians." *Journal of Library Administration* 49, no. 4: 383–400. doi:10.1080/01930820902832538.

King, David Lee, and Michael Porter. 2007. "Collaborating with Wikis." *Public Libraries* 46, no. 2: 32–35.

Love, Mark, and Scott Norwood. 2007. "Finding Our Way as 'Embedded Librarians'." *College and Undergraduate Libraries* 14, no. 4: 87–93. doi:10.1080/10691310802128369.

Luo, Lili. 2010. "Web 2.0 Integration in Information Literacy Instruction: An Overview." *Journal of Academic Librarianship* 36: 32–40.

Matthew, Victoria, and Ann Schroeder. 2006. "The Embedded Librarian Program: Faculty and Librarians Partner to Embed Personalized Library Assistance into Online Courses." *EDUCAUSE Quarterly* 29, no. 4. www.educause.edu/EDUCAUSE+Quarterly/EDUCAUSEQuarterlyMagazineVolum/TheEmbeddedLibrarianProgram/157422.

Mott, Jonathan. 2010. "Envisioning the Post-LMS Era: The Open Learning Network." *EDUCAUSE Quarterly* 33, no.1. educause.edu/EDUCAUSE+Quarterly/EDUCAUSEQuarterlyMagazineVolum/EnvisioningthePostLMSEraTheOpe/199389.

Owens, Rachel. 2008. "Where the Students Are: The Embedded Librarian Project at Daytona Beach College." *Florida Libraries* 51, no. 1: 8–10.

Petit, Joan, and Amanda Click. 2010. "From Lectures and Quizzes to Wikis and Blogs in the Library Classroom." Session presented at the LOEX Annual Conference, Columbus, Ohio. May 1. http://prezi.com/xvw0joxucpom/from-lectures-and-quizzes -to-wikis-and-blogs-in-the-library-classroom/.

Stern, Danielle M, and Michael D. D. Willits. 2011. "Social Media Killed the LMS: Re-Imagining the Traditional Learning Management System in the Age of Blogs and Online Social Networks." In *Cutting-edge Technologies in Higher Education*, edited by Charles Wankel,1:347–373. Bingley: Emerald Group Publishing. www.emeraldinsight .com/books.htm?issn=2044-9968&volume=1&chapterid=1906605&show=abstract.

Sullivan, Elizabeth, John Millard, Katie Gibson, Arianne Hartsell-Gundy, Amy Thornley, and Eric Resnis. 2010. "Re-purposing and Rethinking Social Networking in the Learning Environment." *Journal of Interactive Instruction Development* 22, no. 1. www .salt.org/jiidtoc.asp?key=141319.

Tadros, Marlyn. 2011. "A Social Media Approach to Higher Education." In *Cutting-edge Technologies in Higher Education*, edited by Charles Wankel, 1:83–105. Bingley: Emerald Group Publishing. www.emeraldinsight.com/books.htm?issn=2044 -9968&volume=1&chapterid=1906605&show=abstract.

Tumbleson, Beth E., and John J. Burke. 2010. "When Life Hands You Lemons: Overcoming Obstacles to Expand Services in an Embedded Librarian Program." *Journal of Library Administration* 50, 7/8: 972–988. doi:10.1080/01930826.2010.489 002.

Twitter. 2011. "One Hundred Million Voices." *Twitter Blog*. September 8. http://blog .twitter.com/2011/09/one-hundred-million-voices.html.

99

My Info Quest
A National Text Reference Message Service

Lori Bell, Lili Luo, and Tom Peters

In spring 2009, staff at Alliance Library System (now RAILS—Reaching Across Illinois Library System) decided to expand its services by offering text message reference. Alliance Library System/RAILS is a multitype library system with hundreds of libraries in Illinois. Although many member libraries already offered collaborative chat reference service via QuestionPoint in 2009, none of them were offering text message reference collaboratively or individually.

Alliance Library System had always served as a leader in the area of collaborative virtual reference. It launched the first 24/7 academic virtual reference service in 2001 in Illinois, working with the then North Suburban Library System, a partnership that was to become the foundation of a statewide virtual reference service. Eight years later, the consortium again was looking at ways to expand its outreach. In tough economic times, a collaborative service for text-based reference made sense to the staff. They approached Altarama, a text message reference vendor, regarding the provision of software for a six-month trial period from July until December 2009. Next, invitations and announcements were sent to a variety of library groups and placed on electronic discussion lists. Staff wanted to recruit libraries in as many time zones as possible to provide more extensive service coverage. Online meetings and demos were held to introduce the service and answer questions. The service had a soft launch in July 2009, followed by a larger push and marketing effort for September 2009.

The Alliance Library System wanted to provide a nationwide, eventually international, text message reference service so that more hours of service could be offered without asking libraries to staff the service more than two to three hours per week. With a nationwide and eventually international service, there would be libraries located across multiple time zones, therefore providing more coverage and the ability to offer a wider variety of service hours. With a variety of libraries participating, reference expertise and coverage expanded, which benefited all types of libraries. The common thread for participating libraries was the ability to offer a high-quality service for many hours per week—many more than any library could provide on its own. At first, the only requirement for libraries to contribute was time for training, staffing the desk two hours per week, and attending advisory meetings. The service was fully funded from the Handheld Librarian online conferences through registration proceeds. Beginning in 2011, the cost per library was $399, the consortial price of the Mosio's Text a Librarian service. Participating libraries are located all over the United States, from the West Coast to the East Coast and the Midwest in between. The most difficult part of the service is coordinating the scheduling of all these libraries and the decision making on shared policy issues that needs to take place for a collaborative service.

During the first year, there were approximately sixty libraries of all types across the country participating in the service. Libraries chose to participate because they would have the ability to offer a new service with fewer time demands, less risk, shared expertise, shared coverage, lower start-up and ongoing expenses, and many of the other benefits a collaborative service offers participants.

There were very few problems even among different types of libraries. There was a lot of discussion about evolving guidelines and policy decisions; however, most of the participants agreed on the majority of these items. The service turned out to be very successful in a number of ways for participating libraries. Libraries were able to find out if their community members would use such a service, the types of questions they would ask, and if they wanted to continue with the consortium, go on their own, or discontinue the service. Libraries that decided to continue were willing to pay the cost—$399 per library per year for Text a Librarian—a substantial discount from Mosio's normal prices. The libraries were happy with the quality of service their users were receiving and the amount of time required for the service, two hours per week. Figure 7.1 provides a look at the My Info Quest patron website.

The service was managed by Alliance Library System until May 2010, when the state consortium underwent major budget cuts and staff changes. At that time, the administration of Info Quest was transferred to Mary-Carol Lindbloom, executive director of the South Central Regional Library Council. For the first six months,

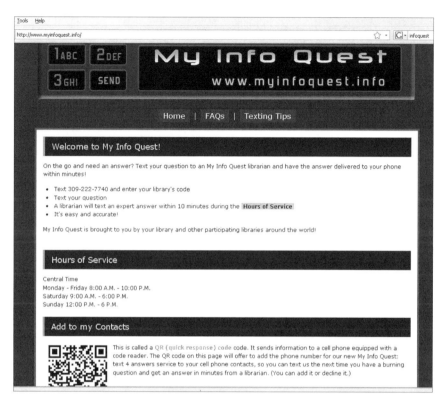

FIGURE 7.1
My Info Quest Website

there was no charge for the service, as Altarama and PeopleWhere donated use of their software for the project. However, during the summer of 2010, librarians from the Alliance Library System decided to explore other text messaging options. They viewed and evaluated demos from a number of vendors and selected Text a Librarian, which they started using in January 2011. This software was selected by the majority for the ease of use, the number of libraries already using the software, the statistics package, and the fact that the software was tailored for the service and did not require any revision to meet the needs of the group. The software was also ideal for service by a consortium. Text a Librarian was working with several consortia and had tailored the software so it worked ideally with groups of libraries in identifying and queuing questions. The software continues to evolve and provide new features that are ideal for groups, including questions first going to the patron's home library before becoming available for answering by the consortium. During the first eighteen months of the project, approximately sixty libraries of all types across the country participated in the project. In January 2011 when libraries had to start paying for the software, the number of participating libraries declined to about thirty.

TECHNOLOGY

The only things a person needs to use the My Info Quest service are a mobile phone, an active service plan, and an information need, which may take the form of a factual question (When does the library open today?), a request for advice (What is the best way to do X?), or a request for an opinion (Do you think Team X or Team Y will win the big game?). Currently there are approximately eight-five active mobile phone service plans for every hundred people in the world. As a result, the potential population served by a SMS-based text reference service is rapidly approaching the entire population of the world. Most of the world's population, however, does not yet know that the My Info Quest service exists. That is a marketing problem. If they did, all they would need is a device, a service plan, and an information need to access our service.

To participate in My Info Quest, the service providers—oftentimes libraries but sometimes individual librarians—need to have a device capable of running a modern browser and Internet connectivity. The Text a Librarian system from Mosio (www.textalibrarian.com), which currently powers the My Info Quest service, is browser-based. There are many computing devices capable of running browser software and connecting to the Internet—desktop computers, laptops, netbooks, tablets, smartphones, and so on. It is conceivable that even certain dedicated portable e-readers, such as the Nook and the Kindle, could be used in a pinch to provide the My Info Quest service. Practically, however, to achieve a good turnaround time on incoming questions (we strive for an average of ten minutes), a service provider needs a computer capable of running at least two browser windows reasonably well. One window is used to present the TAL interface, where questions are received and answers are provided, and another browser window to search the Web for information. Generally speaking, the technology required to use the My Info Quest service is now quite common, affordable, and easy-to-use. Figure 7.2 provides a sample question and answer.

Multimedia messaging service (MMS) almost certainly will replace SMS in the provision of reference services to PP ICEs (personal and portable information, communication, and entertainment appliances), although it does raise the

How You Respond

Click Answer Button

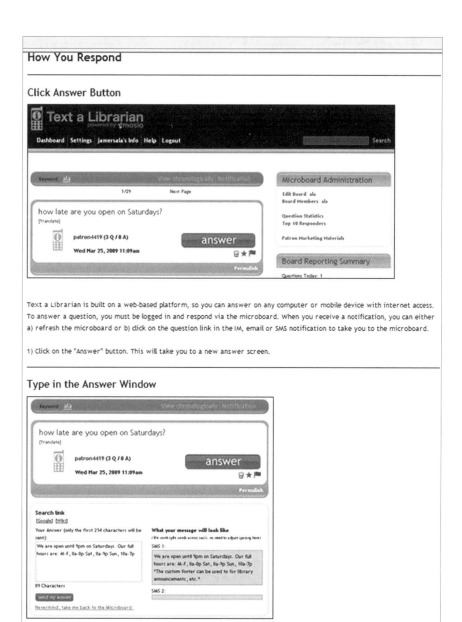

Text a Librarian is built on a web-based platform, so you can answer on any computer or mobile device with internet access. To answer a question, you must be logged in and respond via the microboard. When you receive a notification, you can either a) refresh the microboard or b) click on the question link in the IM, email or SMS notification to take you to the microboard.

1) Click on the "Answer" button. This will take you to a new answer screen.

Type in the Answer Window

FIGURE 7.2
Text a Librarian Question Response

FIGURE 7.3
My Info Quest Google Groups

technology bar a bit. (The My Info Quest service cannot currently handle MMS messages, but we are planning for that enhancement.) The user of the service, for instance, would need to have at least one camera embedded in their PP ICE to be able to express an MMS-based information need. An example we often discuss during online meetings of the My Info Quest advisory group is a person taking a walk in the woods who encounters a plant that she suspects is poison ivy. She pulls out her smartphone, takes a snapshot of the plant, and sends the photo as a MMS message to the My Info Quest service, asking if this plant is indeed poison ivy.

Other technologies are used to support the My Info Quest service. These include a website, a web conferencing service for online meetings, a calendaring service that holds the "desk" schedule, and e-mail discussion groups for asynchronous communication among the participating organizations, service providers, other stakeholders, and fellow travelers. The service website is hosted by South Central Regional Library network and maintained by Lori Bell, coauthor of this chapter, and staff at South Central. The web conferencing service we currently use for online meetings is GoToMeeting provided by the South Central Regional Library System. We currently use Google Calendar to construct and update the reference desk schedule, and we use Google Groups to host the various e-mail discussion groups, as shown in figure 7.3.

TRAINING AND MONITORING

All training and orientation sessions for new service providers are held online using web conferencing software, currently tcConference from Talking Communities, Adobe Connect, or GoToMeeting. Most training sessions are recorded and archived, so that others can view and listen to a training session as the need and opportunity arise. Training sessions rarely take more than one hour and consist of librarians from participating libraries. These sessions cover how to use the software to answer questions, as well as policy and procedural issues. Online group training provides for interaction and brainstorming among the participating librarians.

KEEPING IN CONTACT / ONLINE MEETINGS

The My Info Quest advisory group meets approximately once per month, usually for about an hour, and almost always online using web conferencing software. Because My Info Quest is a grassroots effort, members of the advisory group are not appointed or elected. Any interested individual currently affiliated with one of the member organizations—including the several "rogue" librarians involved in the service, who essentially are organizations of one—are welcome to attend and participate in these online meetings. Barbara Galik from Bradley University in Peoria, Illinois, usually facilitates these meetings. We use a scheduling service, such as Meet-O-Matic (www.meetomatic.com), to poll all the interested individuals about good dates and times for future online meetings.

Using web conferencing software for these online meetings has distinct advantages over telephone conference calls. First and foremost, it is easy and inexpensive to make full recordings of these meetings and archive them on the Web. With service providers spread across at least four time zones and with busy schedules, no matter what date and time are chosen for a live online meeting, there always is a significant portion of interested individuals who have schedule conflicts. The recordings of meetings archived on the Web enable them to circle back at their convenience and listen and view recent online meetings. The session recordings are created locally, edited if needed, and uploaded to a web server. The audio recording in the form of an MP3 file can also be presented as a stand-alone audio recording, for people who want to just listen to a meeting—perhaps while they commute to and from work—without seeing the text chat, presentation slides, and co-browsing activities.

Another advantage of holding online meetings using web conferencing software rather than telephone conference calls is the management of voice transmissions. We have configured the online meeting room to operate in "walkie talkie" mode, meaning that only one microphone is active at any given time. Participants cannot talk on top of one another. If a person wishes to speak, he simply clicks on an icon in the software to raise his hand and request to speak. This technological configuration results in very orderly, civil meetings, and it creates an audio recording that is sequential and easy to understand. Even when the group is discussing a contentious issue, shouting matches never erupt because the online meeting room has been configured so that they cannot.

The group has had to make a number of ongoing decisions about the service and how different issues will be handled. One such decision was whether to use Wikipedia as a credible reference source. After a discussion, a vote was taken as to whether or not this was a credible source for the service. Approximately 50 percent of participants voted that it was credible, and 50 percent voted they did not think it was credible. The group ended up deciding that it would be up to the discretion of the librarian on duty to decide whether or not to use Wikipedia.

Another decision was whether to provide personal telephone numbers of people who could be located from apparently reputable and reliable sources on the Web. At first the group had decided not to give out this information. Later this issue was discussed because if the information is freely available on the Web, why not provide it to patrons? Some libraries had a policy that they could not legally provide this information. In the case of requests for personal information freely available on the Web, it was left to the discretion of each librarian to follow the policies of his or her institution.

One of the most challenging aspects of keeping in contact has involved announcing and negotiating shift changes. Although the My Info Quest policies and procedures state that the person whose shift is ending need not stay until the next person arrives, it has become a common courtesy for the person whose shift is beginning to let the retiring person know that she is "on the desk."

SCHEDULING

During the first six months of the project, PeopleWhere (www.webclarity.info/products/peoplewhere/) generously donated their scheduling software to the

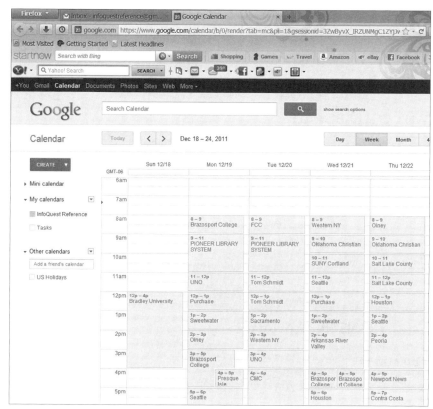

FIGURE 7.4
My Info Quest Google Calendar Schedule

project. Although the software was very powerful and effective, the group decided not to continue with it for 2011. Each library was required to staff the desk two hours per week. Some libraries that were able to do more have done so. The schedule is done for January through May; June through August; and September through December. About six weeks before the schedule is to start, participants send the project coordinator three times they could work the desk. These are put on Google Calendar, which is accessible to all participants (fig. 7.4).

MARKETING MY INFO QUEST

Each library is expected to market the service to their community. There is a marketing/website committee that oversees the project website at http://

myinfoquest.info. The committee has also developed press releases, flyers, business cards, and other marketing tools for each library to edit and use for promoting the service.

WHY COLLABORATE?

The benefits of collaboration may seem obvious, yet in 2012 many libraries are still providing their own individual SMS reference service. A service like My Info Quest can help libraries with stretched budgets and staff to offer virtual reference during more hours without having to staff the desk every hour themselves. Start-up costs are also shared. Text a Librarian gives participating libraries a substantial discount. As far as professional benefits, there is an increase in staff expertise, since reference skills and knowledge are shared among libraries.

CHAT TRANSCRIPT ANALYSIS

Questions

Since its launch in July 2009, My Info Quest has received an average of 780 questions per month. The questions can be grouped into two basic categories: local library related and nonlocal library related. The former refers to questions about patron's local library; for example, questions about a book or film that the library owns, the library's resources, and the library's policies, procedures, and services. About 13 percent of all questions fall under this category.

Among the nonlibrary-related questions, the majority (70 percent) are those that require a single answer, consisting of a specific and definitive piece of information. Katz (2001) defines this type of questions as *ready reference questions*. For example:

- what is a receding hair line?
- what is the difference between green red and yellow bell peppers?
- when was fax machine invented? Thanks!
- how old was albert instine when he died
- what are the hours for graphic flesh in Bloomington, IL.?
- what does Wodaabe mean?

- will Marengo, Illinois get a lot of snow this winter?
- how do u make a milkshake?

Occasionally, there are questions (about 9 percent) that cannot be answered with a particular piece of information and require a rather comprehensive answer too lengthy for the texting medium. Thus, responses to such questions usually consist of information sources (e.g., websites, books, periodicals, or referrals) that patrons can review and synthesize to ultimately formulate their own answers. Here are a few examples of such questions:

- what does it mean when it burns when you pee?
- what is the reason for each country having its own currency?
- I was curious as to what are the details and terms of the new health care bill
- why is it that when a group of women are around each other for a while their menstrual periods sync?

The rest of the questions are of miscellaneous nature.

Overall, My Info Quest's question patterns are consistent with what has been already reported in the literature—patrons seem to be aware of the limitations of texting as a communication venue and tend to use it for questions that require a brief and straightforward answer (Giles and Grey-Smith 2005, Hill, Hill, and Sherman 2007, Kohl and Keating 2009, Pearce 2010, Weimer 2010).

Answers

Since the majority of My Info Quest's questions are ready reference questions, most of the reference transactions do not involve a comprehensive reference interview and tend to be simple and short. About 75 percent of all transactions comprise only two messages (one question and one response), and another 21 percent contain three to five messages, and only a small number (4 percent) includes more than five messages.

When answering patrons' questions, there are three major constraints:

1. When My Info Quest was using Altarama's SMS Reference as the gateway software to route patrons' texts into an e-mail account, each message could not exceed 320 characters (two text messages). If an answer exceeds this

limit, the rest of the answer would be truncated and not seen by the patron. We still adhere to this general guideline.

2. Not every patron has access to the Internet on their cell phone. Thus, they find it inconvenient when being referred to a website for information. For example, a patron seeks information about the lyrics of a song, but it is too long to fit in one response. The librarian then refers the patron to a website that has the full lyrics; however, the patron texts back, complains about the lack of Internet access, and expresses the wish to receive the lyrics via texting. The librarian sends the lyrics in multiple responses in order to meet the patron's need.

3. Not every patron has unlimited texting. In the aforementioned example, if the patron has unlimited texting, receiving multiple texts would not incur any additional cost; but if he doesn't, the cost of texting could be a concern.

Given these constraints, librarians have to be able to strike a good balance of being concise and informative when composing their answers. There are some strategies that can help them achieve this balance. For example, they can use character counters, such as the built-in option in Microsoft Word; URL shorteners, such as Bitly (https://bitly.com); and common abbreviations to help them keep their messages within the limit. It is important that librarians understand how comfortable patrons feel communicating via texting and thus respond to their questions in the same fashion.

LESSONS LEARNED AND WHERE TO GO FROM HERE

My Info Quest has proved to be a successful virtual reference service with steady traffic. There are several things we have learned from this collaborative experience. The first is software selection. Text reference service can be delivered in different ways, such as via cell phone, using free text-to-e-mail applications like Gmail, or using commercial software that allows processing text messages using a computer application. When choosing the proper software, libraries need to consider budget, staffing and usability needs. For example, during My Info Quest's pilot period, when we used Altarama's SMS Reference for service delivery, we identified a few challenges. One was the lack of a mechanism to "claim" a question to avoid two people working on it simultaneously; another was the difficulty in associating patrons' phone numbers with their local libraries. Thus, when the pilot period ended, we evaluated a few other software options and decided on Mosio's Text a Librarian to better meet other service needs.

Training is an important component in launching any new service and should include not only software training, but also training on the nuances, user expectations, and etiquette of the communication medium: texting. Texting has its constraints and advantages as a communication venue, and librarians need to be aware of this to develop a better understanding of how it is used by patrons for communication in general and for reference service in particular. Being familiar with the texting culture, lingo, and etiquette can help librarians more easily assist patrons with their questions. Several helpful sites are NetLingo (www.netlingo .com) and Lingo2word (www.lingo2word.com).

As a self-initiated and self-organized collaborative effort, My Info Quest has faced some challenges in enforcing service policies. In any reference service, it is necessary to have clear policies on the scope of the service, the response time, and the question-answering practice. In a collaborative service, there are additional policy needs; for example, for arranging shift coverage among participating members, and for ensuring consistent service quality by stipulating how to answer certain types of questions (e.g., how nonlocal librarians should hand local library related questions). The loose organizational nature of My Info Quest makes it difficult to monitor the enforcement of these policies. Thus it is important to increase policy awareness through training sessions, sending out periodical reminders, and using auxiliary tools such as effective scheduling software. A strong and dedicated leadership team also plays an important role in establishing and communicating policies to members of the consortium, as well as monitoring service quality.

One service issue that has arisen involves making sure that all service providers understand the context of the needs and technology available to the patron. For instance, many users of this service are using dumb mobile phones and thus do not have immediate access to the Web. As a result, merely sending a URL in response to their question is not immediately helpful. Another example involves the distinction between street or mailing addresses and directions. Most users who ask for information about the location of something (a motel or a library, for instance) are asking for directions, not for the street or mailing address. They are en route to that place and want to know how to get there. For example, one time a person asked for the location of the San Francisco City Hall. The service provider quickly found the mailing address on the city hall's website and sent it as the response.

The patron then clarified that they needed directions, such as streets to take and cross streets to watch for as they approached their destination.

Library participants do not agree on every policy or procedure developed. In these cases they are discussed and decide upon at the advisory group meeting with a vote if necessary. Sometimes, an issue remains unresolved. Participants could not agree whether or not to use Wikipedia. There was extensive discussion concerning the pros and cons. A vote was taken, but it was a tie. The issue was resolved in trusting each librarian on the desk to make his/her own decision about using Wikipedia as a source.

To plan for the future, My Info Quest will focus on the sustainability of the service and getting more libraries to participate and fine-tuning the development of reference services on the mobile platform. Text message reference service will not go away with the increase in the use of smartphones. Texting is still an effective way to ask a question and get an answer.

REFERENCES

Giles, Nicola, and Sue Grey-Smith. 2005. "Txting Librarians @ Curtin." Paper presented at Information Online 2005 conference, Sydney, Australia. February 1–3. http://conferences.alia.org.au/online2005/papers/a12.pdf.

Hill, J. B., Cherie Madarash Hill, and Dayne Sherman. 2007. "Text Messaging in an Academic Library: Integrating SMS into Digital Reference." *The Reference Librarian* 47, no. 1: 17–29.

Katz, William. 2001. *Introduction to Reference Work (8th ed.).* Columbus: McGraw-Hill.

Kohl, Laura, and Maura Keating. 2009. "A Phone of One's Own: Texting at the Bryant University Reference Desk." *College and Research Libraries News* 70, no. 2: 104–106, 118.

Pearce, Alexa. 2010. "Text Message Reference at NYU libraries." *The Reference Librarian* 51, no. 4: 256–263.

Weimer, Keith. 2010. "Text Messaging the Reference Desk: Using Upside Wireless' SMS-to-E-mail to Extend Reference Service," *The Reference Librarian* 51, no. 2: 108–123.

AskColorado
A Collaborative Virtual Reference Service

Kris Johnson

In previous chapters you have learned about a variety of Web 2.0 technology offerings for providing virtual reference services as well as the evolution of VR service at individual institutions. This chapter will focus on cooperative virtual reference, from the perspective of one of the longest-running statewide cooperative services: AskColorado.

Offering continuous service since September 2003, AskColorado has been providing virtual reference (VR) or chat reference service to Colorado's digital information seekers during a time of tremendous flux in the library and information technology fields. Started before technologies like instant messaging (IM) were popular, and through the shift to social media technologies such as Facebook and Twitter and the coinage of Web and Library 2.0 monikers to designate the new information frontier, AskColorado has continued to exist, change, and grow. Colorado is unique in that it is one of only a dozen or so states to ever offer statewide online reference service to patrons via "cooperative reference service"

Cooperative Virtual Reference

"Cooperative reference service is a process through which information assistance is provided by referring the user, or the user's queries, to staff at another institution according to a system of established procedures. Cooperative Reference is understood to mean any type of cooperation through any modes of communication." (RUSA, 2007) (see the sidebar). During this time, other state- or province-wide cooperative virtual reference (VR) services have been formed, later to be dissolved, often with little fanfare, publicity, or documentation. The discontinuation of nine VR services, including three cooperative services, was profiled by Radford and Kern in 2006.

Today, AskColorado remains one of the oldest statewide VR services in the country, and now comprises two distinct but partnering services via two website portals: AskColorado (www.askcolorado.org) and AskAcademic (www.askacademic.org), the latter which serves academic customers from academic member libraries in Colorado as well as other states. The organization's full title is now the AskColorado/AskAcademic Virtual Reference Cooperative, but will be referred to in the rest of this chapter simply as ASK.

This chapter will discuss the formation of ASK as well as its selection and use of vendor-based chat reference software. Chat reference software has been used since inception and continues to be used at present, despite the massive changes in technology offerings since 2003, many of which have been profiled in previous chapters of this book. ASK staff and membership have often been questioned by professionals in the library field how the emergence of the Web 2.0 technologies—especially free or nearly free IM programs such as Meebo (when it was available) or LibraryH3lp—have affected the cooperative. In particular, they want to know if a library is using social software or IM to deliver reference—does it still need a cooperative service like ASK? The fact is, ASK has continued, even as libraries research and experiment with 2.0 technologies to communicate with customers. Why is this, and what factors contribute to the continued longevity and success of the collaborative? What can you learn from ASK to apply as a blueprint for starting your own cooperative service (statewide or other)? This chapter will address these questions, describing the genesis of AskColorado, lessons learned from and changes made in the service over the years, technology used from inception to the present, and an explanation of the decision-making process related to technology selection.

How It All Began: The Inspiration

One of the primary things to consider when starting a VR service is staffing. How many hours can you afford to offer on your new service? Do you have an extensive staff and budget to allow you to provide service all day and into the night (or 24/7)? Early on you will realize that staffing, not technology, will be your greatest expense when offering such a service. Libraries in Colorado realized this *very* early on—from the beginning, in fact. So let's start at the beginning . . .

The inception of ASK ties directly into the vision statement for the Library and Information Technology Association LITA:

> . . . exploring and enabling new technologies to empower libraries. LITA members use the promise of technology to deliver dynamic library collections and services. (LITA, 2011).

Colorado librarians in the early 2000s quickly became aware of and tied together two relatively new trends: 1) the public's increasing leaning toward 24/7 service availability, especially online, in all sectors of life; and 2) new library software being introduced to the profession—live chat, a technology that libraries could use to "talk" to patrons using computers and the Internet using chat technology. The librarians could easily relate to the former, being twenty-first-century citizens themselves. Imagine *not* being able to buy gasoline or shop online at your favorite retailer any time of the day or night! The latter trend, the chat software, although something new, was something that excited them, and was something they could possibly link to the first trend in order to provide a new, dynamic service to patrons 24/7. But how to make such a service a reality? Colorado librarians understood and valued the importance of offering service to patrons electronically, in real time, but without "hours," that is, 24/7. They also knew the only way to do this was to collaborate. No library in the state was wealthy enough to offer a 24/7 service alone, and all knew that in this century, to remain relevant in the eyes of the public, the service must always be available, because people today may work 'round the clock and do not want to think about "open" and "closed" hours.

The end result was that on Sept. 2, 2003, the AskColorado service launched as a 24/7 service available to anyone in the state of Colorado, but with participating libraries staffing no more than ten hours per week for a single library. How did the libraries make this happen?

Getting Detailed

As in most situations in the library profession, in order to get from idea to implementation, task forces and committees were formed, and meetings were held! Details about the inception of AskColorado can be found in my article "Back to the Future" (Johnson 2010). The sidebar outlines a rough time line of events that occurred.

Suffice it to say that the end result of a lot of grassroots efforts by librarians in the state of Colorado led to the formation of a cooperative virtual reference library

Time Line for AskColorado/AskAcademic

2000–2001: Chat reference software is offered by library vendors

Early 2001: Colorado librarians express interest in software and virtual reference

Late 2001: The now defunct Colorado Resource Sharing Board (CLRSIAB, or RSB) charges the Colorado State Library (CSL) with formally investigating the level of interest in virtual reference in Colorado.

Spring 2002: CSL holds two statewide library discussion forums, resulting in a groundswell of interest in the topic.

April 3, 2002: RSB authorizes the creation of a collaborative virtual reference committee (CVRC.) This committee (comprised of librarians around the state from multiple library types and led by the CSL) was charged with continuing to examine the issues related to collaborating on virtual reference on a statewide basis, to investigate different models of virtual reference, and to make recommendations to RSB about which model should be adopted in Colorado and how to proceed with organizing and funding the effort.

Summer 2002: CSL hosts a national collaborative virtual reference symposium, with the goal of educating Colorado librarians about collaborative virtual reference and what was already occurring nationwide (www.webjunction.org/cvrd-2002).

July 29, 2002: CVRC agrees to start formal process of creating a collaborative and discusses what committees should be formed to support the project, including: steering, needs assessment, software, evaluation, policies and procedures, funding, marketing and public relations, and quality control and training

August 2002: RSB recommends CSL apply for Library Service and Technology Act (LSTA) grant monies to launch the service.

service called AskColorado, with centralized support as well as LSTA (Library Service and Technology Act) federal grant monies through the Colorado State Library, and staffing and financial contributions coming from libraries across the state joining as member libraries.

The early organizational and funding structure of ASK remains today: The cooperative is analogous to a food co-op or public radio: it is member and grant supported. Member libraries "join" ASK by signing a letter of agreement and

October 28, 2002: CSL issues a request for information (RFI) to software vendors.

November 2002: CVRC conducts a needs assessment survey to determine Colorado library e-reference current offerings and potential interest in collaborative service. Also, CSL and RSB send a letter to all library directors in the state explaining the possible new collaborative and the funding model (a combination of federal grants and contributions from joining libraries), and asking that commitment-to-participate letters be returned by December 16, 2002.

Late December 2002: Thirty libraries return their commitment-to-participate letters.

January 2003: CSL submits the LSTA grant proposal.

April 16-17, 2003: Vendor software demos begin (the software selection process is highlighted in more details further in the chapter).

May 2003: CSL receives the LSTA grant. Also, CVRC conducts a technology survey of participating libraries. The survey was conducted to aid in the software selection.

July 2003: A cooperative coordinator is hired, the software license is signed, and software training is conducted.

August 2003: The website is established, schedules are established, and details are finalized for the service launch.

September 2, 2003: The service launches.

October 2003: The marketing push begins.

119

committing to a modest financial donation, based on a sliding scale, via staffing, or both. The Colorado State Library also contributes by continuing to provide federal grant monies, a full-time coordinator, and other organizational infrastructure. More information about library membership can be found at www.askcolorado.org/info/libraries.html. Today ASK continues to be funded and operates in the same way; most important, through its member support and governance. Librarians from member libraries set the policies, members select the software, and members govern. In fact, the original objective established by the cooperative is still in place today and forms the foundation for the collaborative, statewide nature of the service:

> Colorado libraries are *collaborating* to provide a 24/7 online chat reference service that efficiently and effectively meets the information and learning needs of Colorado residents. (From AskColorado's staff intranet)

To summarize, the early organizers of ASK knew that sharing costs on a statewide level would translate into savings in management, training, software selection, licensing, implementation, and maintenance, and more, with the availability of the new vendor-based chat software making such a collaborative service possible. Readers may learn from the time line of events outlined in the sidebar, but what worked for ASK may or may not work for other groups or individuals. The process of establishing a VR service is not as step-by-step as the process for selecting an ILS, creating a digital asset management system, or planning some other IT-based service. Readers are also encouraged to consult several well-written guides for launching and maintaining VR service, including Kern (2009) and RUSA (2010) for general virtual reference service, and RUSA (2007) for services that are collaborative in nature. However, the final section of this chapter will outline lessons learned and advice to others interested in establishing a VR service, based on ASK experiences over the past eight years.

ASK IN 2011

Skip ahead eight years. In fiscal year 2011–2012, the ASK cooperative consists of thirty-five public libraries, twenty academic libraries, and twelve special libraries who field referral questions via e-mail. There are approximately two hundred librarians trained to staff the service, with librarians from member libraries staffing the service twelve hours per day Monday through Friday, 8 a.m. to 8 p.m., and eight hours on Saturdays. All other off-hours are covered by an after-hours service located in Colorado and run by ASK. Over the years, ASK librarians have handled more than 325,000 sessions with customers.

The ASK organization continues to offer chat reference service just as it did in 2003, but ASK has not remained stagnant, nor is it the same service that it started as. Over the years the organization has undergone a series of changes, including:

- Bringing into the academic queue libraries from outside Colorado
- Rebranding and securing the domain name AskAcademic
- Starting its own after-hours librarian service
- Selecting a new chat software from a nonlibrary vendor (to be discussed in detail further in this chapter)

As mentioned previously, the ASK organization is member governed. All major decisions are made using member library input and in many cases voted upon by the librarians that comprise its committees. A full list of all the changes the cooperative has made since inception in 2003 is included in the sidebar.

Changes in AskAcademic/AskColorado since Inception

2003 Service launched. Two queues available, general and Spanish.

2004 Two more queues available: An academic queue borne out of general queue and a queue for K–12

Offered companion Live Homework Help service

2005 Discontinued Live Homework Help service

2006 Started Live Help Queue for state government

2007 Cooperative continues to grow with new member libraries joining, but no major changes made

2008 Rebranded: new logo, tagline, and website

Closed Live Help Queue

Added an academic library from Texas (University of North Texas) to academic queue

2009 Selected new software from a nonlibrary vendor

2010 Implemented new software from InstantService, later called ATG Live Chat (now known as Oracle Live Help on Demand)

Launched AskAcademic.org domain (www.askacademic.org)

Expanded and branded the academic queue; added another Texas academic library, Austin Community College

Discontinued the Spanish service queue

Created staff intranet using Drupal

Started the ASK After-Hours service to staff evenings, nights, and weekends

2011   Created modified widgets (for embedding on libraries' web pages) allowing easier patron entry to the service

Expanded AskAcademic again with addition of two more Texas libraries as well as a campus in Missouri (part of Colorado Technical University)

Started pilot project answering questions for first "client"—Jones International University

Added second client library—CSU (Colorado State University)–Global University

One significant change worth highlighting in detail was the software selection process, where we switched from using software from a library chat vendor to a public sector "live help" program from a nonlibrary vendor. This process will be detailed below.

TECHNOLOGY SELECTION

At their core, VR services are human- (not technology-) based organizations. This cannot be emphasized enough. Many VR services have started and failed because of a focus primarily on the glitz—the technology—to the exclusion of all other considerations. If only one piece of advice could be offered to others seeking to start a VR service, fix a VR service, or start a VR cooperative, it would be this: do not look at the venture as one centered solely on technology, and instead focus on the human aspects first. For example:

- Why do you want to offer the service?
- What is your service philosophy?
- What will your policies and procedures be?
- Who will staff the service, and what hours will you be open?

Libraries may learn from ASK's blueprint for success. In addition, as mentioned previously, several well-written guides for launching and maintaining virtual reference services already exist. The key is to not look at technology as the solution to any perceived problem, or as the only factor to consider when determining whether to start a service. There are many factors to consider and technology is an important one, but it is not the only one.

Having said that—and again focusing on LITA's vision of using "technologies to deliver dynamic library collections and services"—the remainder of this chapter will focus on software technologies selected and used by the ASK cooperative.

The initial chat software selected by the ASK Cooperative was from LSSI (Library Systems and Services Inc.), later sold to Tutor.com. The cooperative used Tutor.com's Ask a Librarian software, as well as their after-hours librarian service, Librarians by Request, until February 2010, when it began using software from a nonlibrary vendor, a period of nearly six and half years. However, during this time, the cooperative actively kept abreast of changes in technologies and evaluated the available options as they changed from year to year.

The initial software selection process in 2003 evaluated chat reference software from four library vendors: Docutek, 24/7, LSSI, and OCLC QuestionPoint. From the beginning, major factors in the selection of a software vendor for ASK revolved not only around the technology and what it could and could not do, an exhaustive list of desires was listed in the RFI, but companion services offered from the vendor, including an after-hours staffing service and full-time Spanish virtual reference librarian services. The ability to offer Spanish virtual reference service to ASK customers was a very high priority when forming the cooperative, and remained a high priority over the years. However, basing the software selection process on this "adjunct" service was hindering the cooperative's ability to truly select the best software available, as will be explained later. Starting in 2003 and continuing to the present, the cooperative evaluated and compared chat software vendor offerings in 2004, 2005, 2006, 2007–2008, and 2009–2010.

> In 2004 the cooperative evaluated chat software from these vendors: MCLS 24/7 Reference, Digi-Net Tech E-Librarian, Docutek VRLplus, OCLC QuestionPoint, RightNow, Desk-top Streaming, and Live Assistance.

> In 2005 the cooperative evaluated: Digi-Net Tech E-Librarian, Live Assistance from LiveAssistance, OnDemand Basic/Enhanced from Convey Systems, QuestionPoint 24/7 Reference from OCLC, Timpani SB Chat/Timpani SB Contact Center from Live Person, Virtual Reference ToolKit from Tutor.com, and Docutek VRLplus.

> In 2006 the cooperative evaluated: Docutek VRLPlus, Tutor.com, and OCLC QuestionPoint.

Each year (2004–2006) the evaluation process was conducted by a software selection subcommittee comprised of librarians from the member libraries. These librarians would test available software, conduct literature reviews, and interview librarians using the various technologies at other libraries across the country. The first year, a very detailed list of specifications and features was included in the RFI sent to vendors. Each year the list of specifications and features became shorter and less specific as the group realized sticking to one defined list of criteria was cumbersome and often not relevant; they found comparing virtual reference software more similar to comparing apples to oranges, rather than comparing Braeburn apples to Gala apples. Quite a bit of time was spent in these endeavors, and a recommendation was then made to the steering committee. Each year the steering committee chose to continue with Tutor.com as the vendor for the cooperative, despite recommendations from the software subcommittee that some available technologies were better from a technological standpoint. Again, after-hours service availability and a focus on providing Spanish service were key criteria in the selection process during these years.

In 2007, the software selection subcommittee asked the steering committee for guidance in an effort to not expend energies evaluating software options that would continue to be passed over due to the emphasis on services beyond the technology. That year the steering committee crafted a document outlining their priorities, including the statement

> While the software plays a major role in the selection process, it is not the only component considered. Other considerations include a back-up reference service, a reference service in Spanish, price, and vendor responsiveness/customer service.

Included in their list of priorities were:

- 24/7 coverage, including after-hours librarian service
- 24/7 reference service in Spanish

Therefore, in 2007 the software selection subcommittee only seriously evaluated OCLC QuestionPoint and Tutor.com because those vendors included software as well as backup/after-hours service and Spanish options. Again, after the 2007–2008 evaluation, the steering committee opted to continue with Tutor.com.

The next round of evaluations occurred in 2009–2010. By this time the availability of quick instant messaging (IM) options such as Meebo and LibraryH3lp were rapidly being deployed by libraries—generally not by consortia, but as a service for individual libraries, several ASK member libraries included. ASK member libraries started asking questions about these new technologies and the possibility of using them cooperative-wide. In addition, they started questioning why the Tutor.com software did not seem to be keeping up technically with changes happening in industry as well as the new Web 2.0 environment. Tutor.com had been nonresponsive to technology feature requests submitted by ASK over the years, leading to some restlessness amongst the members and a stronger desire than in previous years to seriously consider changing software.

Meanwhile, the ASK coordinator, while responsible for minding the overall health and welfare of the cooperative, overall project management, and day-to-day care and feeding, had also been tracking the technology trends and watching what other libraries and cooperatives were doing—or not doing—as the technologies changed from year to year. Seeing a whole new world of technology passing the cooperative by, the coordinator finally decided it was time to present an ultimatum of sorts: continue to focus on offering Spanish service to the exclusion of all other technology trends and societal considerations, or move Spanish service down the list of priority features in order to open the software selection process up to more contemporary software options. The cooperative listened, and the steering committee agreed that placing an emphasis on offering Spanish service for so many years, with yearly statistics showing dismal usage numbers, had hindered the cooperative's technological flexibility.

Therefore, for the 2009–2010 software evaluation process, Spanish service would no longer be a priority, and the software selection subcommittee was given the option to evaluate a variety of software vendors otherwise unavailable to the group. During this process the subcommittee evaluated software from:

- Altarama
- InstantService
- LibraryH3lp
- OCLC
- Ohio/Oregon cooperative (using the Spark IM platform)
- Mosio
- Tutor.com

The choices were narrowed down to four finalists: VRLPlus, Reftracker, and Refchatter from Altarama Information Systems (a library vendor); InstantService (a nonlibrary vendor); OCLC QuestionPoint (a library vendor/cooperative); and

Ohio/Oregon (two statewide cooperatives collaborating to program and host Spark, an IM software from Jive Software). All four options offered features key in a collaborative VR service setting, and which were generally not available from free IM services or Web 2.0 social media services, including the ability to create unlimited librarian log-ins; offer unlimited number of queues simultaneously staffed by multiple librarians; having multiple librarians logged in and online simultaneously; storage of chat transcripts; sophisticated statistical module; and the loading and use of scripted messages.

In October 2010, the Software Selection Subcommittee chose InstantService as its #1 software choice. InstantService was a private sector company based in Seattle, which was later acquired by Art Technology Group (ATG) and was subsequently acquired by the Oracle Corporation. At that time, the InstantService software was used by only one other statewide virtual reference cooperative, Ask a Librarian in Florida. Although this software decision required the cooperative to undergo very significant changes, the subcommittee saw numerous advantages to this option that had the potential to offset the changes in very positive ways:

Cost savings. The quoted monthly price was significantly less than the previous vendor, Tutor.com. InstantService was comparable in price to OCLC and Altarama, but much less than choosing the Ohio/Oregon option.

No contract lock. InstantService did not require the cooperative to commit to a one-year contract. The cooperative needed only to give 60 days' notice prior to discontinuing service.

Stability. In all the subcommittee's testing of software and discussions with the Florida cooperative, the group believed this software to be much more stable than the offerings from library vendors.

Expanded compatibility. InstantService was compatible with multiple operating systems and browsers, on both the librarian and patron side. Library vendor offerings had some restrictions in this area.

Communication options. In addition to traditional chat technology, Instant-Service offered a built-in e-mail feature, as well as one-on-one IM for librarian to librarian use, and a chat room in which all librarians logged in at a particular time could communicate with each other.

Referral integration. The software offered the possibility of folding in referral library communication with patrons directly into the software instead of the current method used, which incorporated outside e-mail systems, resulting in cumbersome and error-prone tracking.

From start to finish, the software selection process took approximately eight months. Other groups may work faster or slower depending on numerous factors. Consortia wishing to implement software selection themselves are encouraged to do the following:

1. Test other services from other libraries and consortia to see what their software looks like from the patron perspective.
2. Contact key individuals at other libraries and consortia and ask them what they like about their current software.
3. Contact software vendors and ask for literature and other "specs" related to their software.
4. Do a literature review. One word of warning, however: software is evolving faster than the library profession's ability to publish its literature in a timely fashion. Details about software you read in the published literature may, in fact, be drastically out of date, and the software could have changed since publication. Just be cautious.
5. Test as many software options as you have resources to do so. If your resources are thin, notice what software is used by the majority of libraries or cooperatives and just test those. If you have more resources, expand the number of technologies you test. The more you know, the better you'll be able to make the best decision for your cooperative.
6. Ask for quotes from vendors. Compare the quotes to what you've learned in your research and testing. Sometimes your selection will not be based on the lowest quote. As mentioned previously in this article, comparing chat software options can be like comparing apples to oranges.

As mentioned previously, selecting the current software option required the cooperative to undergo several changes, one very significant. Because InstantService was a nonlibrary vendor, they naturally did not offer a 24/7 backup staffing service as did those from Tutor.com or OCLC QuestionPoint. In 2010, ASK contracted for 105 hours per week, or 5,460 hours per year, of staffing from Tutor.com. Therefore,

FIGURE 8.1
Ask Colorado Patron Interface

selection of InstantService required ASK to develop its own backup staffing service in order to continue to offer chat service during the hours the member libraries were not staffing the service. Figure 8.1 shows the patron view for AskColorado.

CURRENT TECHNOLOGY FEATURES

ASK has been using the InstantService software since February 2011. The software has since been acquired by Oracle Corporation and is presently called Oracle ATG Live Help on Demand. Despite two acquisition processes since implementation, the cooperative has been immensely satisfied with the software. Oracle Live Help on Demand is entirely web based, both for administrators as well as librarians. The software is hosted by Oracle, which is very good about sending notices about server or software maintenance upgrades. Thus far, the software is stable and rarely results in disconnects from patrons. Figure 8.2 provides an image of the AskColorado widget.

○ **Available now.**

Type your question here, then click "Ask Now!" to send.

Ask Now!

Got Questions?
AskColorado

FIGURE 8.2
AskColorado Widget

Administrator

From an administrative standpoint, the software is perfect for a librarian or administrator with no major programming background or skills. Queues can be created in a manner of minutes, allowing member libraries to have their own unique chat queues, if needed. The cooperative as a whole manages three main queues (academic, K–12, general), but new queues can be created on the fly without consulting the vendor and without any major programming knowledge. The software also contains a robust analytics component. Statistics can be generated in real time in order to monitor service at any given time of the day. Examples of the statistics console are shown in figures 8.3 and 8.4. As

FIGURE 8.3
Chat Activity Report Module

ORACLE® Live Help On Demand

Reports

Agents
View customer activity for one or more selected agents.

Chat Activity	View agent-specific customer chat activity counts over a chosen time period
Chat Transcripts	View agent-specific chat transcripts over a chosen time period
Chat Queue Distribution	View agent-specific chat queue distribution over a chosen time period
Mail Activity	View agent-specific customer mail activity counts over a chosen time period
Mail Messages	View agent-specific mail messages over a chosen time period
Mail Queue Distribution	View agent-specific mail queue distribution over a chosen time period
Login Summary	View summary information for agent login times
Availability Summary	View summary information for agent availability

Departments
View customer activity for one or more selected departments.

Chat Activity	View department-specific customer chat activity counts over a chosen time period
Chat Transcripts	View department-specific chat transcripts over a chosen time period
Chat Queue Distribution	View department-specific chat queue distribution over a chosen time period
Mail Activity	View department-specific customer mail activity counts over a chosen time period
Mail Messages	View department-specific mail messages over a chosen time period
Categories	View categorized chat and mail customers
Mail Queue Distribution	View department-specific mail queue distribution over a chosen time period
Exit Surveys	View department-specific exit survey responses

Customer Lookup
View detailed information for a specific customer.

Chat Customer	View details on a specific chat customer based on various customer criteria.
Mail Customer	View details on a specific mail customer based on various customer criteria.
Originated Agent Mail	View details on a specific originated agent mail based on various criteria.

FIGURE 8.4
Administrative Report Module

compared to the previous software from Tutor.com, there is no delay of one to several hours in order to pull transcripts or generate statistics. Statistics are available nearly up-to-the-minute.

The same process stands for librarian log-ins. New log-ins take one to two minutes to create and become available to a librarian, and settings can be adjusted on a librarian-by-librarian basis. For example, some academic librarians like to cover our public queues. Access can be easily given to those librarians. Individual representatives from member libraries can have access to the statistical module. Their log-ins can be modified to gain this access on a request-by-request basis.

Librarian

From the librarian standpoint, the ease of use of the software far surpasses the previous software. The software has many of the familiar features present in chat software from library vendors including new patron alerts, the basic chat feature, web page pushing, and the ability to preload scripted messages and URLs. In addition, the Oracle Live Help on Demand software offers a spell checker, an IP locator, and tokens, which allow the software to automatically insert patron data into scripted messages. One feature the librarians especially like is the ability to upload a photo or avatar of themselves that will display in the patron interface. The librarians feel this features adds a human touch to the interaction and helps to facilitate more friendly and open communication.

Another feature is an industry standard color-coding system that employs the colors white, yellow, and red to get the librarian's attention as a patron waits longer for service. The color changes from white to yellow at the one-minute mark, then from yellow to red once the patron has been waiting for more than five minutes. Another key feature is the ability to field multiple sessions simultaneously so patrons do not have to reach the five-minute mark. Librarians can field multiple patrons with ease using a tabbed system in the agent console as shown in figure 8.5. The administrator can set a limit on how many simultaneous patrons a librarian can accept, anywhere from one to ten. A librarian can simultaneously e-mail and chat with a patron, can send files as attachments via the chat, and can e-mail transcripts. As mentioned above, librarians are rarely disconnected from patrons

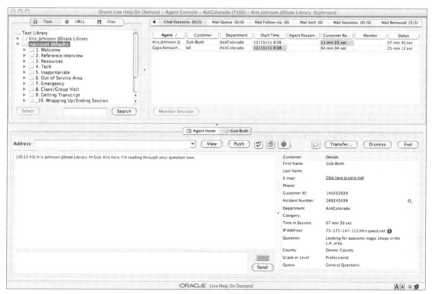

FIGURE 8.5
Agent Console

due to software issues. However, they are sometimes faced with a disconnected transaction due to a local issue, either on the librarian or the patron side. When this happens, the software has a nice feature in which the session is not lost or disconnected, but rather rerouted back to the queue it came from, for pickup by another, or the same, librarian.

LESSONS LEARNED AND GOING FORWARD

Librarians in Colorado discussing virtual reference in the early 2000s could never have predicted the course of the cooperative over the subsequent years. The cooperative is fortunate to have persisted and thrived during this time, but many factors ended up contributing to make this so, and each year has presented challenges to overcome. The following can be considered lessons learned and advice to others wishing to start a collaborative virtual reference service:

Collaborate and mean it. The core to survival of any type of library collaborative is to participate in the collaborative as a full member and to the fullest extent. Do not join a collaborative expecting to be serviced. Provide your service to the collaborative in the form of input, feedback, committee work, advocacy, and more.

Communicate. If you're happy with the way things are going, communicate this internally and externally. If you aren't happy, let the group know why. ASK has several ways in which members can communicate including committees, e-mail lists, a staff intranet, meetings, annual letters to directors asking for feedback and providing kudos to staff, an annual workshop, and more.

Pay attention. Read all communications from the collaborative. Do your research. If you can't find an answer to a question you have, ask someone in the collaborative. Do not make decisions about your participation in a collaborative based on guesses, hearsay, or incorrect information.

Value training. To participate in a collaborative VR effort, more training is necessary than starting a service at a single library. There is more information to know about member libraries, the policies of the cooperative, and the chat software. One key to the overall success of a collaborative is proving consistent, high-quality service, and the one way to achieve

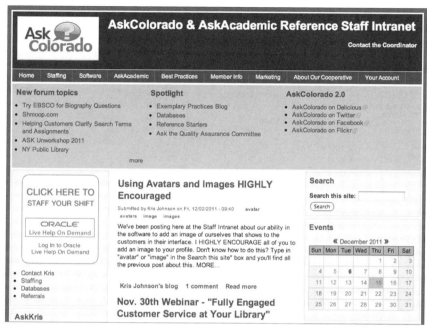

FIGURE 8.6
ASK Staff Blog

this is through training and ongoing continuing education. ASK has a basic training requirement for all librarians of four hours, conducted by the coordinator, but most librarians realize after this training that they've only scratched the surface regarding the knowledge they will need. ASK offers additional training upon request, holds an annual workshop, and communicates best practices via documentation and a staff intranet in an effort to supplement the basic training session. An example of the staff intranet is shown in figure 8.6.

Promote the service. Do you want your library's patrons to use the VR service? Then it will be up to your library to conduct its own PR and marketing to make this a reality. Don't expect the collaborative to drive your patrons to the service just because you joined and your name is listed at a website somewhere. Even though your library may not be in charge of all the details of software maintenance, training, and the like, it is your library's job to drive your patron traffic to the service. Jefferson County Library's Ask Us page is shown in figure 8.7 as an example of a library that has a high-quality promotion page.

133

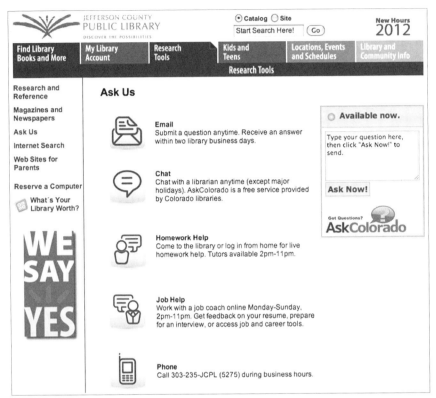

FIGURE 8.7
Ask Us Site—Jefferson County Library

Don't measure success based on traffic alone. Use of your VR service is important, but don't base all your decisions on the value of the service on metrics alone. Tying into the point above, other measures of success for VR services can often be intangibles, difficult to measure, such as your librarians improving their reference knowledge due to participating in the service, which they can apply at your library; the overall image of libraries in the mind of the public; and more.

As mentioned above, the cooperative has faced many challenges over the years. The biggest challenge we face is unhappiness by select member libraries and a loss of libraries from time to time. Often, libraries have left the cooperative without providing notice of their intentions to leave, or having asked questions about issues they were unhappy with or concerned about. In several situations, libraries have left, citing a detailed list of their dissatisfaction, but only after the fact. While feedback is important and appreciated, unfortunately for the collaborative, in several of the situations the feedback cited inaccurate information. These libraries only discussed their concerns internally. Had they collaborated, communicated, and paid attention, as advised in the points above, the libraries could have made a better informed decision, perhaps choosing to continue with the cooperative once points were clarified or explained.

Some libraries have left the collaborative not based on dissatisfaction per se, but because of the emergence of the Web 2.0 technologies, especially free or nearly free IM programs such as LibraryH3lp (www.libraryh3lp.com). Primarily, large academic libraries have left and started their own internal VR services. Apparently this works better for them, and they having the funding and staff to provide adequate hours, but it is noted that none of these libraries offer service 24/7 as does ASK. Other academic libraries, such as the Auraria University Library (Denver), have started their own internal service while remaining a member of ASK, valuing the dual roles each service plays in reaching their students (Evans, McHale, and Sobel 2010). Auraria believes that a library can use social software and maintain an internal IM to deliver reference, but that this does not preclude their participation in ASK (fig. 8.8).

135

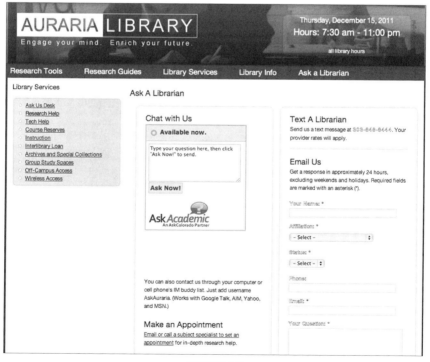

FIGURE 8.8
Ask a Librarian Site—Auraria Library

Finally, for many libraries in the state, ASK is the only service they would consider providing to their patrons. For the most part, Colorado is a rural state. Many of our libraries simply don't have the funding or the staffing to provide many hours of virtual reference on their own, but they value this service for their rural patrons. For them, ASK is their only option—and as described in the introduction to this chapter, the reason the cooperative was formed in the early years. Further details about the cooperative ethos necessary and exemplified by ASK can be found in "Collaborative Virtual Reference Really Does Work, but It Takes a Tribe" (Johnson et al. 2012). All patrons are given a link to an exit survey, and results are used to help us maintain excellent service.

The reason the ASK cooperative continues to exist and thrive today is because the majority of the participating libraries participate like they mean it. They value the service, and they do what they need to do to keep the service running. Cooperatives thrive on mass, and the more libraries that participate, the more stable the cooperative will be.

REFERENCES

Collaborative Virtual Reference Symposium. 2002. www.webjunction.org/cvrd-2002.

Evans, Lorrie, Nina McHale, and Karen Sobel. 2010. "Apples and Oranges: Creating A Hybrid Virtual Reference Service with Proprietary Chat Reference Software and Free Instant Messaging Services." In *Reference Renaissance: Current and Future Trends.* Edited by Marie L. Radford and L. David Lankes, 163–173. New York: Neal-Schuman.

Johnson, Kris.2010. "Back to the Future: The AskColorado Collaborative Virtual Reference Cooperative." *Colorado Libraries* 35, no. 1. http://coloradolibrariesjournal.org/?q=node/27

Johnson, K., P. Farrell, K. Laughlin, P. Mascarenas, and A. Sieving. 2012. "Collaborative Virtual Reference Really Does Work, but It Takes a Tribe." In *Leading the Reference Renaissance: Today's Ideas for Tomorrow's Cutting Edge Services.* Edited by Marie L. Radford (in press). New York: Neal-Schuman.

Kern, M.K. 2009. *Virtual Reference Best Practices: Tailoring Services to Your Library.* Chicago: American Library Association.

LITA. 2011. "About LITA." www.ala.org/ala/mgrps/divs/lita/about/index.cfm.

Radford, M. L. & Kern, M. K. 2006. "A Multiple-Case Study Investigation of the Discontinuation of Nine Chat Reference Services." *Library & Information Science Research* 28, no. 4:521–547.

RUSA. 2007. "Guidelines for Cooperative Reference Services." *Reference and User Services Quarterly,* 47, no. 1: 97–100.

RUSA. 2010. "Guidelines for Implementing and Maintaining Virtual Reference Services." *Reference and User Services Quarterly* 50, no. 1: 92-96.

Suggested Reading

VIRTUAL REFERENCE: GENERAL

Bridgewater, Rachel, and Meryl B. Cole. 2009. *Instant Messaging Reference: A Practical Guide*. Oxford: Chandos House.
   Focused specifically on instant messaging, including technologies available, assessment, marketing, privacy issues, and best practices.

Coffman, Steve, P Michelle Fiander; Kay Henshall; Bernie Sloan. 2003. *Going Live: Starting and Running a Virtual Reference Service*. Chicago: American Library Association.
   Practical advice for beginning or supplementing a virtual reference service. Nice chapter on marketing.

Dalston, Teresa R., and Michael Pullin, eds. 2007. *Virtual Reference on a Budget: Case Studies*. Columbus, Ohio: Linworth.
   Selling the idea of virtual reference to others, low cost options, and considering time constraints of libraries. Variety of libraries considered.

Hirko, Buff, and Mary Bucher Ross. 2004. *Virtual Reference Training: The Complete Guide to Providing Anytime, Anywhere Answers*. Chicago: American Library Association.
   Examines core competencies for consistent service, learning activities, and tools for developing a training program at your library.

Kern, Kathleen M. 2009. *Virtual References Best Practices*. Chicago: American Library Association.
   Provides tools and strategies to evaluate and enhance virtual reference services.

Kimmel, Stacey, and Jennifer Heise, eds. 2003. *Virtual Reference Services: Issues and Trends*. Binghamton, NY: Haworth Information Press.
   Reviews issues, trends, and practices in VR, across all library types. Offers practical advice and suggestions, covers tools and marketing,

Lankes, R. David, Joseph Janes, Linda C. Smith, and Christina M. Finneran, eds. 2004. *The Virtual Reference Experience: Integrating Theory into Practice*. New York: Neal-Schuman.
   Examines patrons, librarians, policies, legal issues, surveys, and training.

Lankes, R. David, Eileen Abels, Marilyn White, and Saira N. Haque, eds. 2006. *The Virtual Reference Desk: Creating a Reference Future*. New York: Neal-Schuman. Considers training, staffing, performance standards, evaluation, working with diverse groups and, building collaborations and networks.

Lankes, R. David, Scott Nicholson, Marie L. Radford, Joanne Silverstein, Lynn Westbrook, and Philip Nast, eds. 2008. *Virtual Reference Service: From Competencies to Assessment*. New York: Neal-Schuman.
Provides real-world case studies and examples to demonstrate tools and techniques.

Lipow, Anne Grodzins. 2003. *The Virtual Reference Librarian's Handbook*. New York: Neal-Schuman.
Explores reference policies workflow, communication strategies, and marketing.

Meola, Marc, and Sam Stormon. 2002. *Starting and Operating Live Virtual Reference Services: A How-to-Do-It Manual for Librarians*. New York: Neal-Schuman.
Discusses six key steps to consider when beginning or enhancing a virtual reference service. Includes basic and advanced service models.

Radford, Marie L., and R. David Lankes. 2010. *Reference Renaissance: Current and Future Trends*. New York: Neal-Schuman Publishers.
Discussion of the current state of virtual Reference. A variety of tools examined and service models explored.

Ronan, Jana Smith. 2003. *Chat Reference: A Guide to Live Virtual Reference Services*. Westport, CT: Libraries Unlimited.
Practical guide for starting or enhancing an existing virtual reference service with case studies. Only academic libraries discussed but transferable to other types of libraries.

Ross, Catherine Sheldrick, Kirsti Nelson, and Marie L. Radford. 2009. *Conducting the Reference Interview: A How-to-Do-It Manual for Librarians*. 2nd ed. New York: Neal-Schuman.
Tips and techniques for conducting reference interviews across a variety of tools. Includes information on working with diverse groups of patrons.

RUSA. 2010. *Guidelines for Implementing and Maintaining Virtual Reference Services*. www.ala.org/rusa/sites/ala.org.rusa/files/content/resources/guidelines/virtual-reference-se.pdf.
Comprehensive and helpful information.

RUSA. 2004. *Guidelines for Behavioral Performance of Reference and Information Service Providers*. www.ala.org/rusa/resources/guidelines/guidelinesbehavioral.
Valuable training and assessment tool. Updated to included virtual reference.

RUSA. 2003. *Professional Competencies for Reference and User Services Librarians*. www.ala.org/rusa/resources/guidelines/professional.
Vital information for training, mentoring, and evaluating reference staff.

West, Jessamyn, ed. 2004. *Digital Versus Non-Digital Reference: Ask A Librarian Online and Offline*. Binghamton, NY: Haworth Information Press.
Variety of topics including starting, maintaining, assessing, and ending virtual reference services. Also discusses outsourcing of services, collaborative endeavors, and cultural/language barriers.

WEBSITE USABILITY

Campbell, Nicole, ed. 2001. *Usability Assessment of Library-Related Web Sites: Methods and Case Studies*. Chicago: American Library Association.
Case studies provide solid tips and tricks for performing usability studies. Practical application of the top usability testing techniques.

Garrett, Jesse James. 2010. *The Elements of User Experience: User-Centered Design for the Web and Beyond*. Berkeley, CA: New Riders.
Discusses website usability, brand identity, information architecture, and interaction design. Less emphasis on techniques and tools, and more focused on idea generation. Includes discussions about mobile devices.

Gergle, Darren, Scott D. Woods, and Tom Brink. 2002. *Usability for the Web: Designing Web Sites That Work*. San Francisco: Morgan Kaufman Publishers.
Guides reader through process of designing and implementing useable websites.

Krug, Steve. 2005. *Don't Make Me Think: A Common Sense Approach to Web Usability*. 2nd ed. Berkeley, CA: New Riders Press.
Practical advice for both beginners and experts. Readable format.

Layon, Kristofer. 2011. *Mobilizing Web Sites: Strategies for Mobile Web Implementation*. Berkeley CA: Peachpit Press.
Making websites suitable for mobile devices.

Norlin, Elaina, and CM! Winters. 2000. *Usability Testing for Library Websites: A Hands-On Guide*. Chicago: American Library Association.
Basic information on usability testing, web design guidelines, best practices for making change occur, assessment and planning, preparing for testing, and evaluating test results. Practical forms and examples included.

Pearrow, Mark. 2006. *Web Site Usability Handbook*. 2nd ed. Rockland, MA: Charles River Media.
Focus on user-centered design and tools and techniques for usability evaluation.

Redish, Janice. 2007. *Letting Go of the Words: Writing Web Content That Works*. Boston: Morgan Kaufmann.
Strategies, processes, and techniques to develop or update web content in a useable manner.

MARKETING AND ADVERTISING

Barber, Peggy, and Linda Wallace. 2003. "10 Tips for Marketing Virtual Reference Services." Found at www.ssdesign.com/librarypr/content/p070802a.shtml. From 2003, but the ideas are still very valid.

Bell, Lori, and Mary-Carol Lindbloom. 2011. "My Info Quest Marketing Ideas." www.myinfoquest.info/marketingideas2011.doc. A chart of ideas used by libraries in the My Info Quest cooperative. The chart is adapted with permission from AskAwayIllinois.info VR services.

Fisher, Patricia H., and Marseille M. Pride .2009. *Blueprint for Your Library Marketing Plan*. Chicago: American Library Association. Step-by-step guide to develop a marketing plan. Discusses all steps, including implementation and evaluation. Forms and worksheets included.

MacDonald, Karen I., Wyoma VanDuinkerken, and Jane Stephens. 2008. "It's All in the Marketing: The Impact of a Virtual Reference Marketing Campaign at Texas A&M University." University Library Faculty Publications. Paper 30. http://digitalarchive .gsu.edu/univ_lib_facpub/30. Details a recent campaign and includes results and assessment of the marketing endeavors.

Mathews, Brian. 2009. *Marketing Today's Academic Library: A Bold New Approach to Communicating with Students*. Chicago: American Library Association. Advice, tips, and techniques to match user needs with useful services taking into account the lives of students. Focuses on new or underused marketing techniques.

Siess, Judith A. 2003. *Visible Librarian: Asserting Your Value with Marketing and Advocacy*. Chicago: American Library Association. Contents include customer service, marketing, advocacy, and publicity. Real-life tips and examples.

Vilelle, Luke. 2006. "Marketing Virtual Reference—What Academic Libraries Have Done." *College Undergraduate Libraries* 12, no. 1: 65–79. Real-life examples of marketing VR services. Practical ideas for increasing traffic. Applicable to other services.

USER NEEDS ANALYSIS AND SATISFACTION STUDIES

Biblarz, Dora, Stephen Bosch, and Chris Sugnet. 2001. *Guide to Library User Needs Assessment for Integrated Information Resource Management and Collection Development*. Lanham, MD: Scarecrow. Focused on collection management with techniques useful for all types of libraries. Array of techniques, methodology, and data discussed.

Dudden, Rosalind Farnam. 2007. *Using Benchmarking, Needs Assessment, Quality Improvement, Outcome Measurement, and Library Standards: A How-to-Do-It Manual with CD-ROM.* New York: Neal-Schuman.
  Each topic discussed thoroughly. Information on goal setting, staffing, planning, data collection and analysis, and using results. Includes worksheets, forms, and checklists to jump-start the process.

Durrance, Joan C., Karen E. Fisher, and Marian Bouch Hinton. 2005. *How Libraries and Librarians Help: A Guide to Identifying User-Centered Outcomes.* Chicago: American Library Association.
  Discusses the "How Libraries and Librarians Help" outcomes model. Provides user survey examples from libraries that have used the model.

Foster, Nancy Fried Foster and Susan Gibbons, eds. 2007. *Studying Students: The Undergraduate Research Project at the University of Rochester.* Chicago: Association of College and Research Libraries.
  Application of ethnographic techniques and tools to user studies. Helpful content both in terms of doing your own studies and in results that can be transferred to your own institution.

Fox, Robert, and Ameet Doshi. 2011. *SPEC Kit 322: Library User Experience.* Washington: Association of Research Libraries.
  Reports on current and planned user experience projects at member libraries.

Grover, Robert J., Roger C. Greer, and John Agada. 2010. *Assessing Information Needs: Managing Transformative Library Services.* Westport: Libraries Unlimited.
  Information on community information needs analysis. Leads reader through background, methods, data collection, analysis, and interpretation. Includes case study to demonstrate process.

Mathews, Brian. 2009. *Marketing Today's Academic Library: A Bold New Approach to Communicating with Students.*
  Although focused on marketing, Mathews explores ways to determine user needs. Many ideas translate to other types of libraries.

Pantry, Sheila, and Peter Griffiths. 2009. *How to Give Your Users the LIS Services They Want.* London, UK: Facet.
  Information for all library types on strategic planning, user studies, staff training, marketing, and budgeting.

141

KEEPING UP WITH TECHNOLOGY

ALA TechSource (blog).
  www.alatechsource.org

Suggested Reading

Educational Technologies and Libraries
   www.scoop.it/t/educational-technology-and-libraries

Kolabora.
   www.kolabora.com/ reviews of latest technology

Library Success: A Best Practices Wiki
   www.libsuccess.org/index.php?title=Library_Success:_A_Best_Practices_Wiki

Library Technology Guides
   www.librarytechnology.org/

LIBREF-L@Listserv.kent.edu
   (electronic discussion list for reference librarians)

Tame the Web
   http://tametheweb.com/

Technology (blog). *New York Times.*
   www.nytimes.com/pages/technology/index.html

Wired
   www.wired.com

About the Contributors

LORI BELL is a full-time lecturer at the School of Library and Information Science at San Jose State University. She teaches classes in management, social networking, virtual services, mobile technology, and other topics. Bell began teaching full time in fall 2010. Prior to that, she worked at Alliance Library System in various positions, such as director of innovation and director of the Mid-Illinois Talking Book Center for eighteen years. Bell has worked in a variety of other library settings including a medical library, a community college, and several public libraries. She has participated on a number of virtual reference projects, including the first 24/7 collaborative academic project, the Illinois Statewide virtual reference project; the creation of InfoEyes for visually impaired patrons; and most recently My Info Quest, a collaborative text message reference project. She has an MS in library and information science from the University of Illinois and a certificate in distance learning from Western Illinois University.

DARCY DEL BOSQUE is the Emerging Technologies librarian at the University of Nevada–Las Vegas. Her role is to enhance library services through the use of new technologies. Her research interests include the use of technology in libraries and its impact on users. These interests are reflected in two of her recent publications, "Forgotten resources: Subject guides in the era of Web 2.0." and "User failure to find known library items." Del Bosque holds an MLS from Indiana University, an MA from Ohio University, and a BA from the University of Minnesota.

ELLEN HAMPTON FILGO is the e-learning librarian at the Baylor University Libraries. In addition to providing reference and instructional services to students and faculty at Baylor, Filgo designs and creates online instructional materials. Additional interests include how new generations of students are using the Internet and connecting those styles of use with the online resources the library provides. She is also interested in how computer technologies, new media, and Web 2.0 enable people to create their own webs of learning. Filgo is very passionate about virtual reference services. She established and manages the popular Ask a Librarian service at the Baylor University Libraries and led them in being an early adopter of the LibraryH3lp software for virtual reference. She also helped set up her library's Twitter and Facebook accounts. Filgo is the author of "#Hashtag Librarian: Embedding Myself into a Class via Twitter and Blogs," published in *Computers in Libraries* in 2011, and has presented about this unique experiment in virtual reference and instruction at the EDUCAUSE Learning Initiative Annual Conference, LOEX, the Mississippi State University Libraries Emerging Technology Summit, ALA Midwinter, and ACRL. Filgo received her BA in comparative literature from Oberlin College in Ohio in 1997 and her MSLS from the University of North Carolina–Chapel Hill in 2007.

BRIAN C. GRAY is the team leader for Research Services at the Kelvin Smith Library (KSL) at Case Western Reserve University. With a background in engineering, he has long had an interest in using technology to collaborate and provide new services. While at KSL, he has helped to create a Web 2.0 training for library staff, implemented blogs for marketing of library resources and services, and implemented instant messaging and text messaging as reference tools. Since January 2007, Gray has been teaching Web 2.0 and other technologies for the Kent State School of Library and Information Science. He has presented on and written articles about Web 2.0, virtual reference, virtual worlds, or mobile technologies.Gray currently is the webmaster for Library Leadership and Management Association (LLAMA) of the American Library Association (ALA), in which he has implemented a wiki and several blogs for LLAMA. He is also part of the web team for the Academic Library Association of Ohio (ALAO). In 2008, he was the first academic librarian in North America to receive the Thomson Scientific Quantum2 InfoStar Award for his work in using Web 2.0 technologies in the library.

KRIS JOHNSON has been a virtual reference consultant at the Colorado State Library and the AskColorado/AskAcademic (ASK) coordinator since July 2006. She also has extensive hands-on reference and instruction experience from her previous life as an academic librarian, primarily at California State University–Chico, as well as a few other academic institutions in the western United States. Johnson obtained her MLIS from the University of Texas, Austin and is a member of the American Library Association, Special Library Association, Mountain Plains Library Association, and Colorado Library Association. Kris has published previously in the field of library instruction, and most recently has several articles and chapters on virtual reference.

SIDNEY LOWE is the head of Research and Information for the University Libraries at the University of Nevada–Las Vegas. She is responsible for overseeing the various modes of delivery for Lied Library's reference services. Lowe also manages the libraries' government information resources. She spent many years as a paraprofessional library employee before earning her MLIS from the University of North Texas in 2004. Lowe earned her BA in sociology from the University of California–Santa Barbara and also holds a master's degree in public administration from the University of Nevada–Las Vegas.

LILI LUO is an assistant professor at the School of Library and Information Science at San Jose State University, where she teaches courses on reference and user services, and research methods in library and information science. Her primary area of research interest is digital reference, and she has been publishing actively in this area. In 2009, Luo received a two-year grant from Institute of Museum and Library Services (IMLS) to study best practices of texting-based reference service, the newest form of digital reference service. Her other research interests include library education, information seeking behavior, and human-information interaction.

145

TOM PETERS currently serves as the assistant dean for Strategic Technology Initiatives at Milner Library at Illinois State University in Normal. Prior to that, he was the CEO of TAP Information Services, a company he founded in 2003 to help organizations innovate. Peters also has worked at the Committee on Institutional Cooperation (CIC, the academic consortium of the Big Ten universities and the University of Chicago), Western Illinois University in Macomb, Northern Illinois University in DeKalb, Minnesota State University at Mankato, and the University of Missouri at Kansas City. He completed his undergraduate work at Grinnell College, where he majored in English and philosophy. He earned his library science degree at the University of Iowa and an MA in English at the University of Missouri at Kansas City. His library experience includes reference service, library instruction, collection management, information technology, and administration. Peters' current interests include the adoption and diffusion of information technologies in general, e-reading on portable devices, online continuing education opportunities, and mobile library initiatives.

Index